POWER BITES

POWER BITES

CHRISTINE BAILEY AND HEATHER THOMAS

PROTEIN-PACKED & KETO-FRIENDLY
SNACKS AND ENERGY BOMBS

THUNDER BAY
P · R · E · S · S

San Diego, California

CONTENTS

THE RECIPES

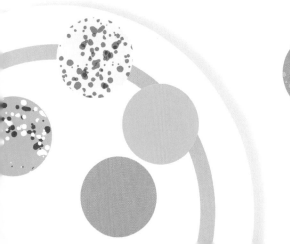

 vegan
GF gluten-free

GETTING STARTED

Here is all you need to know before you check out the recipes. Find out what power bites are and how you can incorporate them into a high-protein, keto, or low-sugar diet. You'll also find information on the ingredients and equipment required.

WHAT IS A POWER BITE?

A homemade power bite is the perfect on-the-go snack for staving off hunger pangs and eating before or after a workout.

Packing a powerful punch for such small snacks, power bites can help you to stay healthy, providing the essential nutrients your body needs while keeping hunger at bay. Eating five or six small meals or "bites" a day can be more effective than consuming two or three large ones.

Power bites come in many forms, but they all have a nutritious combination of protein, carbohydrates, and healthy fats. We have grouped them into high-protein, keto, and low-sugar bites to make it super-easy to find your favorites.

Our high-protein snacks and energy balls are perfect for fueling a workout or satiating hunger. Low in carbohydrates and packed with healthy fats, they can also be included as part of a keto diet.

The keto fat bombs and snacks in this book have been created to be high in fat, moderate in protein, and low in carbohydrates. They will help you to burn more fat for fuel and have been specifically formulated to keep you in ketosis.

We have also created a number of low-sugar and low-fructose power bites, which do not rely on syrups, dates or excess fruits but rather use a range of delicious natural ingredients to provide sweetness without upsetting your blood sugar levels. If you are looking for a snack to pick you up after a workout, to grab-and-go for breakfast or to tackle a mid-afternoon slump, these bites are the perfect sweet hit.

Nice and easy

We've made it super-easy for you by creating delicious recipes that are really user friendly. You don't need to spend hours in the kitchen, nor do you need any special cooking skills. And the equipment you'll require is minimal. All the ingredients are familiar and can be found in supermarkets, delis, and health food stores or bought online.

Nutritional values

Every recipe has its own at-a-glance detailed nutritional analysis, providing you with the information you need, including the numbers of calories, fat and saturated fat grams, carb and sugar grams, and protein grams per bite. This makes it easier for you to calculate your fat, carb, and protein intake. And if you have a snack attack and want to grab something to eat in a hurry, you can check that your power bite is protein-packed, keto-friendly, or both!

WHY HIGH PROTEIN?

A moderate intake of protein is part of any successful balanced diet because protein is essential for growth, helps to repair your body, and maintains great health. A high-protein diet can also help you lose weight because it makes you feel full and can reduce your carbohydrate intake. If you like to work out, protein is essential for gaining and/or maintaining muscle.

Some studies have also suggested that protein is more effective if you spread it out through the day in snacks, rather than eating it all in one big meal.

It can be challenging though to find tasty low-carb, high-protein snacks, as most store-bought snack foods, such as cakes, cookies, pastries, and chips, are packed with flour, starches, and sugar – all the foods you need to keep to a minimum. But don't worry – help is at hand.

YOUR DAILY GUIDELINES

Ensuring you eat enough protein is essential to a healthy diet. Try and make sure you get your protein from a variety of sources.

• **Moderate protein**
The average woman needs at least 50g of protein a day and a man 60g. If you are doing lots of activity or want to build muscle mass, you will need more than this. Some people prefer to use a simple calculation of eating 0.4g of protein per pound of body weight each day.

• **High protein**
A high-protein diet can be up to double this, so about 1g protein per pound of body weight per day. And consuming at least 25–30 percent of your calories from protein has been shown to boost your metabolism and help with weight loss.

NUT BUTTERS

Nut butters are a fantastic healthy way of introducing extra protein into your diet and are surprisingly versatile. They are also keto-friendly and can add flavor and texture, as well as nutrients, to savory power bites as well as sweet ones.

Health benefits

Nuts are among the world's healthiest foods. High in protein and heart-healthy omega-3 and -6 fats, nut butters are low in sugar and carbs but rich in vitamins and minerals. Their polyunsaturated and monounsaturated fat content helps to lower cholesterol and fight inflammation.

Types of nut butters

Many supermarkets and health food stores now sell a range of high-protein, keto-friendly nut butters – but take care. Many of them contain sugar and other additives, so be sure to check the labels carefully.

Almond butter: This has fewer calories and more vitamin E and dietary fiber than other nut butters. Eaten at breakfast time, almond butter can stabilize blood sugar levels for the rest of the day.

Brazil nut butter: Most of the fat content of Brazil nuts is monounsaturated and it helps to lower LDL (bad cholesterol) and raise HDL (good cholesterol).

Hazelnut butter: This is a good source of fiber, vitamin E, minerals, and omega-6 fatty acids, but it only has half the protein contained in peanut butter.

Macadamia nut butter: This is low in saturated fat and contains a variety of healthy vitamins and minerals. It lowers unhealthy LDL cholesterol and blood pressure and controls blood sugar levels. Due to its high fiber content, it is gut friendly and helps to prevent constipation.

Peanut butter: This is the most widely consumed nut butter in the world. It's highly nutritious, especially in protein, vitamin E, and minerals, and available salted or unsalted, plain or with added flavorings, smooth or crunchy. Check the labels and avoid any brands that have added sugar and palm oil.

Pecan butter: This is slightly higher in fat than other nut butters and contains omega-3 and -6 healthy fats, as well as dietary fiber.

While nut and seed butters are now widely available, if you're a big fan of them you may find it's cheaper to make your own nut butters from scratch at home. It's so easy too. On pages 16–17 we have a couple of delicious recipes to inspire you.

NUT BUTTER FLAVORINGS

There are so many ways you can jazz up homemade nut butters. Experiment by adding a wide range of flavorings, depending on whether you want your nut butters to be salty, sweet, spicy, hot, or aromatic. Try the following:

• You can turn any of the nut butters into a choco-nut spread by adding cocoa powder (see page 17). If you want a creamier version, stir in a little almond milk or coconut milk to form a thick chocolate paste.

• Nut butters are also delicious with added superfoods – try lucuma powder or maca powder to give your butter a mild caramel flavor.

• If you like a sweeter nut butter, then add a little dash of yacon syrup, finely ground xylitol, or a few drops of liquid stevia.

• Make use of natural extracts like vanilla. Or add vanilla seeds for flavor and texture.

• There is also no reason why you cannot combine nuts and seeds together.

• Alternatively, try using half unsweetened coconut flakes and half nuts for a creamy spread.

• Sea salt or Himalayan salt.

• Fresh root ginger.

• Try spices for additional flavor, such as cardamom, cayenne, cinnamon, cloves, nutmeg, paprika (sweet or smoked), or za'atar.

• For a spicy-sweet kick, add red pepper flakes, dried chili powder or a dash of a fiery hot sauce, such as sriracha or Tabasco.

• For more tang, grate in citrus zest – lime or orange.

• Cocoa, dark chocolate, espresso powder, or coffee beans will give your nut butter a choc-mocha flavor.

Peanut Butter, page 16

PEANUT BUTTER

MAKES 1LB 2OZ
(500G)

**3½ cups (500g)
shelled raw
peanuts**
**1 tbsp sunflower or
peanut oil**
Sea salt (optional)

PER BITE
Calories: 177kcal
**Fat: 8.5g
(1.8g saturated)**
Carbohydrates: 1.8g
Sugars: 0.7g
Protein: 4.2g

It's so easy to make your own peanut butter, whether it's smooth and creamy or crunchy and nutty. Roasting the peanuts yourself not only enhances their flavor and aroma, but also releases their natural oils. You can make cashew, almond and macadamia nut butters in the same way. Just roast and grind the nuts until you have a creamy paste.

Preheat the oven to 350°F (180°C).

Spread out the peanuts in a single layer on a baking sheet. Roast in the oven for 10 to 15 minutes until golden brown and fragrant. Remove and set aside to cool.

Blitz the peanuts in a food processor until they are coarse and gritty. If you want to end up with a crunchy texture, remove some and set aside.

Add the oil through the feed tube and keep blitzing, stopping occasionally to scrape down the sides of the bowl, until the peanuts release their oils and you have a moist, smooth and creamy paste. Stir in the reserved coarsely ground nuts, if you removed them earlier.

Transfer to a sterilized 18oz (500g) glass jar with a screw-top lid or a Mason jar and keep in the fridge for up to 2 months.

(VE) (GF)

CHOCOLATE HAZELNUT SPREAD

This is really delicious and healthier than most commercial spreads, many of which have added palm oil and sugar. You can use it not only for making fat bombs, cakes, and cookies, but also for spreading on keto cloud bread. And it's gluten-free and dairy-free, making it vegan-friendly.

Preheat the oven to 350°F (180°C).

Spread out the hazelnuts in a single layer on a baking sheet and roast in the oven for 10 to 15 minutes, until golden brown and the skins are loose. Remove and cool.

Wrap the cold hazelnuts in a paper towel and rub and roll them around in it to remove the skins.

Blitz the hazelnuts in a food processor for 10 minutes, stopping occasionally to scrape down the sides of the bowl, until they release their oils and you have a moist, smooth paste.

Add the oil through the feed tube and keep blitzing, then add cocoa, vanilla, and salt to taste. Blitz again, adding sweetener to taste – a few drops at a time.

Transfer to a sterilized 14oz (400g) glass jar with a screw-top lid or a Mason jar and keep at room temperature for 3–4 weeks.

MAKES 14OZ
(400G)

- 3 cups (400g) raw hazelnuts
- 1 tbsp sunflower or peanut oil
- 2 tbsp good-quality unsweetened cocoa powder
- **Few drops vanilla extract**
- **Sea salt, to taste**
- **Liquid artificial sweetener, to taste**

PER BITE:
Calories: 121kcal
Fat: 11.5g
    (1g saturated)
Carbohydrates: 1.5g
Sugars: 0.4g
Protein: 2.9g

WHY KETO?

The keto diet is a low-carb, high-fat diet that shifts your body's metabolism away from carbs. We get most of our energy from carbohydrates (sugar, starch, and fiber) and these are broken down into glucose before being absorbed into the bloodstream. Our bodies utilize the glucose as fuel for all our activities and what we don't burn is stored as fat for long-term energy and, consequently, we put on weight.

Ketosis

A keto diet makes your body more efficient at burning fat for energy. To achieve this you need to reduce your carbs to 5 percent of your daily calorie intake, or 2oz (50g) maximum, which means cutting out most grains, starchy vegetables, fruit, legumes, and sweets. You replace those lost calories with fats, which are turned into an alternative energy source called ketones – molecules that are produced in the liver, from fats, when glucose is limited. Getting most of your calories from fats rather than carbs forces your body to use alternative energy pathways, so it burns fat instead of glucose. Your body enters a metabolic state called ketosis, where ketones are the main sources of energy, not only for your body but also for your brain. This helps to make you feel less hungry and promotes weight loss.

Staying healthy

Research studies have shown that a keto diet is more effective at promoting weight loss than low-fat diets. People following a keto diet not only lose twice as much weight as people on conventional calorie-controlled diets, but they are also more likely to maintain their weight at a healthy level. And because a keto diet makes you feel full and reduces hunger, you are less likely to snack between meals.

As well as helping you to lose excess fat – a factor linked to developing type 2 diabetes – it reduces blood sugar levels and improves insulin sensitivity. It also reduces LDL (bad) cholesterol levels and blood pressure for good heart health.

Mix and match

Because eating the keto way can be quite restrictive, especially if you follow the diet long term, most doctors and nutritional experts agree that you need to eat a variety of foods to ensure you get all the essential nutrients your body needs. A concern is that if you limit your intake of nutrient-rich vegetables, fruits, and grains and eat a lot of high-fat animal products and saturated fat, you may be more at risk of developing some health problems, such as heart disease. The good news is that you can avoid this by focusing more on healthy plant-derived fats, such as olive oil

Granola with Chocolate Drizzle, page 88

and avocado, and oily omega-3 fatty acids found in fish such as tuna, salmon, and mackerel, rather than too much red meat.

Protein

A traditional keto diet advocates a moderate consumption of protein. However, you can increase the amount of protein you eat within a keto diet, which can be a particularly effective approach if you exercise frequently or want to add variety to what you eat. A high-protein keto diet is thought to be just as effective for weight loss. We have included both moderate- and high-protein power bites in this book.

What can you eat?

When you embrace a keto diet to lose weight and boost your health, you need to focus on reducing your carb intake while increasing the fat and protein content of all your meals and snacks. This is why power bites are so important. When you're starting out, you may find it quite challenging to create delicious morsels without carbs, but there are lots of permissible foods that you can mix and match if you know how to do it.

If you struggle to imagine high-energy snacks without bread, cakes, potatoes, and many of the other starchy and sugar-laden ingredients that bulk out your meals, stop worrying. The recipes in this book provide the solution. By using healthy plant-protein alternatives, natural low-sugar sweeteners, and a little cunning and imagination, you can still enjoy many of your favorite snacks.

YOUR DAILY GUIDELINES

All you have to do to meet your energy and nutritional needs while staying in ketosis is to eat the following nutrients in the recommended proportions:

- **High fats**
These should account for approximately 65–75 percent of your daily calorie intake.

- **Moderate/high protein**
This should account for 20–30 percent of your daily calorie intake.

- **Low carbs**
These should account for only 5 percent of your daily calorie intake.

KETO GUIDELINES

Here are some general guidelines for planning and cooking keto-friendly snacks, bites, and meals.

Eat a variety of fat-rich foods

These include vegetable fats, such as nuts, seeds, avocados, extra-virgin olive and coconut oils, as well as oily and white fish, shellfish, organic poultry, red meat, offal, eggs, and dairy. Be sure to avoid unhealthy fats, especially heavily processed hydrogenated vegetable oils and trans fats, which are harmful to heart health. Opt instead for fats from nutrient-dense, organic foods.

Increase your fat intake

Here are some useful tips:

- Cook with butter, olive, or coconut oil
- Serve salads with olive oil and avocado oil dressings
- Drizzle cooked vegetables with melted butter
- Include plenty of eggs in your diet
- Make thin omelet wraps
- Eat at least two portions of oily fish per week
- Use full-fat coconut milk in preference to dairy
- Add olives to salads, wraps, and balls
- Mash canned tuna or smoked salmon with mayonnaise and cream cheese
- Eat chicken, duck, and turkey skin
- Use full-fat butter and cream
- Choose high-fat cheeses

- Eat plenty of nuts and seeds
- Add nut butters to sauces, fat bombs, smoothies, and bakes
- Sprinkle nuts and seeds over salads and bites
- Add avocado to smoothies, sauces, and frozen popsicles
- Roll sweet balls in dried shredded coconut

Choose your protein intake

Moderate- and high-protein keto diets both limit carbohydrate consumption to 5 percent of daily calorie intake. A high-protein keto diet has more protein in relation to fat, which has benefits for those who are very active or older, helping to maintain strength and build and repair muscles. Some people worry this may affect weight loss as, like carbohydrates, protein can be converted into glucose or energy, which is what causes you to come out of ketosis. However, it is thought that these worries are unfounded and a high-protein keto diet can still result in significant weight loss, alongside the health benefits of a reduction of sugar and processed carbohydrates in the diet. Choose a selection of protein-rich foods from the keto traffic lights list (see pages 24–25).

Keep carbs to a minimum

Cut out pasta, rice, bread, grains, beans, legumes, and starchy vegetables. Snack on less fruit, especially ones that are high in sugar. Substitute almond meal, almond flour, and coconut flour for regular flour when baking, and use them as a thickener for sauces and energy bombs. Use vegetables and plant proteins as substitutes for pizza bases (cauliflower), sliders (eggplant) and rice (cauliflower). Use natural sweeteners instead of sugar, honey, agave, and maple syrup for fat bombs, cakes, and cookies.

Cut out highly processed foods

Avoid foods that contain trans fats, flour, and sugar: cookies, cakes, pastries, breaded chicken and fish, sweetened nut butters, breakfast cereals, ice cream, and yogurt. Check the labels on tomato ketchup, barbecue sauce, sweet dipping sauces, and salad dressings – many contain hidden sugar.

Eat low-carb vegetables

Avoid starchy vegetables – potatoes, sweet potatoes, parsnips, rutabaga, beets, celery root, and butternut squash. Choose vegetables that grow above ground, including leafy greens, cabbage, broccoli, cauliflower, and green beans. Too few high-fiber vegetables in your diet could lead to constipation.

Eat a variety of foods

Ensure you get a wide range of essential nutrients, particularly dietary fiber, vitamins and minerals. Have fun experimenting with different ingredients.

Use aromatic herbs and spices

These are not only healthy but a great way of flavoring power bites. You can roll savory cream cheese balls in chopped herbs or spices such as paprika or cayenne pepper. Use ground cinnamon and cardamom for sweet bites.

Staying in ketosis

Once you get into ketosis you have to stay there. Inevitably there will be times when your ketone levels drop or kick you out of ketosis, especially if you're traveling or break your routine. However, if you resume eating your keto-friendly foods as soon as possible you'll get back on track. Here are some tips to help you stay in ketosis.

• Eat unprocessed foods – many processed and packaged foods contain hidden ingredients, such as sugar and carbs.
• Read the labels on packaged foods and learn which to avoid.
• Always have keto-friendly bites and snacks on hand – there are plenty of great recipes in this book.
• If you don't have much time to cook, make bites in batches in advance and freeze for a later date.

KETO TRAFFIC LIGHTS

This at-a-glance table will help you to identify the healthy ingredients you can eat freely, foods you can enjoy occasionally or in moderation, and those you should stop eating.

Grains
Wheat, couscous, quinoa, buckwheat, bulgur, pearl barley, oats, sorghum, millet, polenta, cornmeal, bread, rice, pasta, noodles, cakes and cookies made with sugar and regular flour

Processed foods
Crackers, potato chips, tortilla chips, processed meat, processed cheese, and breakfast cereals

Unhealthy fats
Margarine, corn oil, and trans fats

Sugar and sweeteners
All sugars, honey, agave syrup, maple syrup, and corn syrup

Preserves
Jelly, most chutney (made with sugar), tomato ketchup, honey, and mustard

Vegetables
Parsnips, turnips, potatoes, sweet potatoes, and corn

Nuts
Honey roasted and salted caramel

Fruit
Bananas and grapes

Beans and legumes
Kidney beans, garbanzos, lima beans, cannellini beans, black beans, lentils, and split peas

Vegetables
Butternut squash, carrots, beets, celery root, rutabaga, peas, pumpkin, and zucchini

Sauces
Pesto, salsa, and tomato paste

Fruit
Mango, apples, pears, oranges, lemons, grapefruit, limes, pineapple, and dried fruit

Chocolate
Milk and white

Sweeteners
Yacon syrup and rice malt syrup

Meat and poultry
Beef, pork, lamb, venison, bacon, organic offal, good-quality sausages without additives (preferably organic and grass-fed); poultry (including skin) such as chicken, turkey, duck; lard

Fish
White fish; oily fish such as salmon, tuna, mackerel, herring, sardines, and trout (preferably wild, not farmed)

Shellfish
All

Dairy
Organic free-range eggs and full-fat milk; cheese such as full-fat hard and soft cheeses e.g. cheddar, Brie, mozzarella, goat's cheese, cream cheese and mascarpone; yogurt such as full-fat and kefir; organic full-fat butter, ghee, heavy cream, and sour cream

Vegetables
Peppers, tomatoes, eggplants, asparagus, cucumber, celery, cauliflower, radishes, green beans, snow peas, bok choy, scallions, mushrooms, garlic, lettuce, chilies, broccoli, cabbage, kale, spinach, and Brussels sprouts

Fruit
Avocados, olives, kiwifruit, melon, berries (in moderation) such as raspberries, strawberries, blueberries, blackberries

Nuts and seeds
Nuts such as pecans, Brazils, macadamias, walnuts, coconut, hazelnuts, peanuts, almonds, and unsweetened organic nut butters; nut flour substitutes such as almond meal, almond flour, and coconut flour; nut milks, especially full-fat coconut milk and coconut cream; seeds such as pumpkin, sunflower, flaxseeds, chia seeds, tahini, and sunflower seed butter

Oils
Avocado oil, extra-virgin olive oil, coconut oil, and sesame oil

Herbs and spices
All

Sauces and condiments
Thai fish sauce, béarnaise sauce, soy sauce, Tabasco, mayonnaise, salt, pepper, mustard, vinegar, lemon and lime juice, wasabi paste, and horseradish

Chocolate
Dark chocolate (more than 70 percent cocoa solids) and unsweetened cocoa powder

Sweeteners
Stevia, xylitol, erythritol, and monk fruit

WHY LOW SUGAR?

To stay in ketosis, you have to cut back on your carb intake, which means substantially reducing or eliminating sugars in your diet. Even if you are not following a keto diet, we are all becoming more aware these days of the harmful effects sugar has on the body. But you don't have to give up sweet snacks. We have created a whole chapter of healthy low-sugar power bite recipes to swap in when you are craving a sweet rush or need a fast energy hit.

Added sugars (such as sucrose and many syrups) contain plenty of calories, but no essential nutrients – they are what we term "empty" calories. Not only are they damaging to our waistline and to our teeth, but more and more research is now linking a high intake of these sugars to many long-term health conditions, such as cancers, autoimmune diseases, diabetes, inflammatory conditions, heart disease, and brain disorders. Before sugar enters the bloodstream from the digestive tract, it is broken down into two simple sugars: glucose and fructose. Glucose can also be produced by our bodies and used as a fuel, but fructose is not produced in any significant amount and our bodies can only metabolize it through the liver.

This is not a problem if we eat only a little, such as in a piece of fruit, or if we have been exercising hard and our bodies can quickly use it up for energy. However, the trouble is that many foods contain so much fructose from added sugars that the body cannot use it and it is then converted into fat in the liver.

Sugars are found naturally in foods such as fruits, vegetables, and grains, and as lactose in milk products. The main concern, however, is around added sugars, usually in the form of sucrose (table sugar), syrups, and high-fructose corn syrup. It is estimated that half of our sugar intake comes from everyday foods such as ketchup, dressings, and bread.

That's not to say you should avoid fresh fruit – especially lower glycemic fruits such as berries, avocado, cherries, and citrus. The glycemic index (GI) measures how blood sugars react to carbohydrate-based food and drink. Pure glucose (100 GI) is used as a reference of scale.

Foods with a low GI, such as most fruits and vegetables, slowly raise blood glucose levels. They are packed with antioxidants, vitamins, and minerals and their fiber content helps slow down the rate at which the sugars are digested and metabolized, avoiding sudden surges in blood sugar. However, dried fruit, which forms the base of most energy balls on the market, is a very concentrated form of sugar and fructose, and it is easy to eat far too much. Some of our recipes include dried fruit, but only a low amount.

KETO-FRIENDLY SWEETENERS

Rather than relying on syrups, sugar, and dried fruit for sweetness, some of the recipes in this book make use of vegetables and fruits that are naturally sweet – for example, pumpkin, carrot, and butternut squash are starchy, sweet vegetables.

Other recipes use whole fruits like apples, pears, and plums or berries. In some cases, you can add sweetness using spices such as cinnamon or powders like lucuma. Where you need more sweetness, here are a few safer options you can try.

Xylitol and erythritol are sweeteners known as sugar alcohols, and they can be used interchangeably. Naturally derived, typically from corn and birch, they are much lower in calories than regular sugar and do not upset blood sugar levels. They are available in granular form and can be used to replace normal sugar in recipes at a 1:1 ratio. Excess xylitol has been known to cause digestive issues in some people.

Stevia is a natural low-calorie sweetener available in liquid or granular form. Extracted from the leaves of the plant *Stevia rebaudiana*, it is incredibly sweet and you need much less of it than regular sugar in recipes, as 1 teaspoon of stevia is the equivalent of 15 tablespoons of sugar. Stevia contains virtually no calories, has a low glycemic index, and is fructose free.

Yacon syrup comes from the yacon tuber, an Andean crop. The syrup tastes a bit like molasses, but has a low glycemic score (between 1 and 5). As it does still contain fructose (around 40 percent), it is best used sparingly and more as a flavoring rather than a sweetener.

Rice malt syrup is made from fermented brown rice and has a lower fructose content but it is still high in calories so again, use sparingly. Check labels to make sure rice and water are the only ingredients. While other syrups, such as maple syrup or honey, can be used instead, these are higher glycemic sweeteners.

USEFUL EQUIPMENT

Power bites are easy to make and you don't need to invest in lots of expensive equipment. However, you might find the following items useful, as they will save you time and effort.

Electric blender: This is useful for blitzing smoothies and whipping up energy balls and fat bombs.

Food processor: You'll need this for making your own nut butters and large batches of power bites. You can chop up the ingredients finely by hand for the recipes, but this can be a time-consuming process.

Handheld electric whisk: If you don't have a blender or food processor, a handheld electric whisk is a great addition to a kitchen and will take all the hard work out of beating power bite mixtures.

Baking sheets: These are essential for baking many savory bites as well as for freezing balls and fat bombs or chilling them in the fridge to firm them up.

Silicone mat: This is useful for baking. Not only is it non-stick but, unlike parchment paper, it's reusable. Use it to line a baking sheet or for making chocolate bark.

Silicone cupcake and muffin molds: These come in different shapes and sizes and they are useful for baking as well as freezing sweet power bites and fat bombs. They're worth the money, as the bites don't stick and you can turn them out easily.

Popsicle molds: Frozen pops are easier to make and turn out with these special molds. Some have built-in sticks, whereas others come with disposable wooden sticks. You can buy them online.

Small ramekins or custard cups: These are perfect for making mini mousses. You can buy them made of glass or ceramic.

Spring-loaded ice-cream scoop: This is useful for shaping frozen power bites, sweet and savory truffles, and parfait balls.

Dehydrator: This allows you to make your own "activated" nuts for a nut butter that is easy to digest, but still delivers on flavor. It certainly isn't an essential tool for making power bites, but a homemade activated nut butter is a fun upgrade for recipes.

Chocolate Ganache Truffles, page 90

Citrus Coconut Truffles, page 102

BASIC INGREDIENTS

DRY INGREDIENTS

Nuts are incredibly nutrient-dense with a good combination of healthy fats and protein. They can also supply essential vitamins and minerals, including zinc, calcium, B vitamins, magnesium, potassium, and manganese.

In many of the recipes that follow, the types of nuts are interchangeable. You can grind them to form a flour as the base of bites or you can use them finely chopped to add texture.

Seeds are equally nutrient-dense and some, such as chia, flaxseed, and hemp seeds, are also rich in the essential omega-3 fatty acids, which are important for heart health, lowering inflammation, and supporting brain function. Ground seeds are readily available or you can grind your own in a blender, juicer, or food processor.

Ground flaxseed and chia seeds are very absorbent and can be used interchangeably with each other but not as a replacement for other seeds or nuts. They are particularly useful to help bind the energy balls.

Dried shredded coconut and coconut flakes (choose unsweetened brands) are simply coconut flesh that has been grated and dried. They are a good source of fiber, manganese, and copper, which supports

energy production. They also contain medium-chain triglycerides – a type of saturated fat the body can use readily for energy.

Rolled oats and gluten-free grains provide a nutritious base in energy balls. Oats are high in fiber, including beta glucans, which have been shown to support immune health and lower cholesterol. With their low glycemic index (GI), oats help balance blood sugar levels, keeping you energized and feeling fuller for longer. Oats are also packed with an array of vitamins and minerals including B vitamins, magnesium, zinc, and manganese.

If you are following a gluten-free diet, make sure you select certified gluten-free oats or use an alternative such as quinoa, millet, buckwheat flakes, or puffed rice.

Coconut flour is a popular gluten-free and paleo-friendly flour, commonly used in baking and recipes. Made from ground and dried coconut flesh, it is low in carbohydrates, high in fiber, and a good source of energizing medium-chain fatty acids. It is highly absorbent: only a small amount is needed and it is ideal for binding the energy balls mixture.

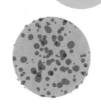

Protein powder and colostrum powder are used in some of the fitness booster recipes in this book. These provide plenty of amino acids to support the recovery and repair of muscles after exercise and help to stabilize blood sugar levels, enabling you to train harder for longer.

Colostrum is the first milk produced by mammals and contains immunoglobulins, antimicrobial peptides and other bioactive molecules including growth factors to support a healthy immune system, aid the growth and repair of tissue, and maintain a healthy digestive tract. Now readily available as a supplement powder, it is popular with athletes before and after training.

If you cannot get hold of colostrum, you could use any protein powder instead – choose plain or vanilla according to taste. To keep the sugar content low, make sure you check your brand for any sweeteners it contains.

WET INGREDIENTS

Fresh vegetables, fruit, and legumes add flavor, nutrients, and moisture to energy balls. For the best results, choose whole fruits and canned beans and legumes, such as garbanzos. You can use these puréed or grated.

Canned unsweetened pumpkin purée and applesauce are easily available or you can simply cook and purée your own. Frozen fruit also adds a wonderful creamy texture to energy balls.

Coconut oil is solid at room temperature, naturally dairy-free and has a delicious creamy texture. Used melted or softened, the oil helps bind the energy bombs and adds a lovely rich taste. Coconut oil is a medium-chain fatty acid and is predominantly made up of lauric acid, known to support immune health.

Coconut milk and cream or almond milk are included in some of the recipes. These naturally dairy-free options add the necessary moisture to the bombs, helping the mixture combine and stick together as well as adding healthy fats to the recipe. By including such fats, you help satisfy appetite and stabilize blood sugar levels, preventing energy crashes during the day.

Tahini (sesame seed paste) is rich in B vitamins, along with many minerals, including magnesium, copper, calcium, phosphorus, manganese, iron, and zinc. It provides amino acids and polyunsaturated essential fatty acids, giving a delicious silky texture.

Nut butters are also used in the recipes. Select those without added sugars or sweeteners and watch the salt content. Better still, make your own from raw unsalted nuts (see pages 13–17). Nut and seed butters can be used interchangeably in all the recipes in this book.

Cacao butter is the natural fat from the cocoa bean. Free from dairy, gluten, and sugar and solid at room temperature, it provides a creamy texture and helps energy bombs to firm up once they are chilled.

FLAVORINGS AND COATINGS

Ground cinnamon gives a lovely warming flavor. There are two different varieties of this spice – Ceylon and cassia. Where possible, choose Ceylon, which is the type associated with health benefits. Cinnamon has a very low GI, making it an ideal natural sweetener. It has also been studied for its benefits in balancing blood sugar and improving insulin sensitivity.

Ginger, whether fresh root or ground, adds a lightly spiced flavor to power bites. For a sweeter addition, use stem ginger, which is sold in jars. Ginger is high in gingerols, a substance that has both powerful anti-inflammatory and antioxidant properties.

Lemon, lime, or orange zest is a great way to add plenty of flavor to your bites. Choose organic unwaxed fruit.

Flavor extracts, such as vanilla and almond, can also be used to give a boost to your power bites. Choose natural extracts, which will have little to no sugar and normally a fresher, cleaner flavor. You can also use pure ground vanilla bean powder or vanilla paste, which are both sugar free.

Raw cacao powder is generally preferred over processed cocoa powder for the recipes in this book, being higher in antioxidants and minerals. It also has a richer, milder taste. But feel free to use the processed version if that is all you have available – you may just need to use a little less.

SUPERFOOD POWDERS

Lucuma powder
Made from Peruvian lucuma fruit that has been dried at low temperatures and milled into a fine powder, this low-glycemic sweetener contains many nutrients including beta-carotene, iron, zinc, vitamin B3, calcium, and protein. It also has a really delicious maple-caramel taste.

Maca powder
A potent root from the Andes in Peru, maca has been used by cultures as a source of nourishment for thousands of years. Referred to as an adaptogenic herb, it has been studied for its ability to help the body adapt to stress. Popular as a superfood to help boost energy and performance, it has a lovely creamy, slightly nutty flavor.

Berry powders
Berries are prized for their nutrient density, and using berry powder further enhances the flavor and nutritional benefits of your bites. Use freeze-dried powders that retain the vital nutrients and flavor of the fresh fruit. You can find berry mixtures or use individual berry powders such as acai. These are low-glycemic fruits that are packed with antioxidants and fiber.

Matcha green tea powder
Made from the whole leaf of the tea plant, matcha powder is packed with antioxidants, including catechins, known for their anti-inflammatory properties. Matcha green tea has been shown to boost metabolism and burn calories, as well as support detoxification, and also boost mood and concentration. As it is concentrated, you will only need one to three teaspoons in most recipes.

Supergreens powders
Chlorella, spirulina, wheatgrass, and barley grass are just a few examples of green superfood powders. Packed with chlorophyll and antioxidants, these help to lower inflammation and support the cleansing and detoxification of the body. Many, such as spirulina, are also rich in amino acids and essential fats, as well as a vast array of vitamins and minerals, making them powerful energizing additions. As supergreens powders are strong in flavor, use sparingly – just half to one teaspoon is normally sufficient.

MAKING ENERGY BOMBS

Many of the recipes in this book are for energy bombs, little nutritious balls of goodness packed with energy, including keto-friendly fat bombs and high-protein energy balls. These energy bombs are very simple to make. Most don't even require any baking and they are the perfect pick-up-and-go snack. Some of the recipes make use of a standard food processor or blender for speed but it's often possible to make them by hand in a mixing bowl, finely chopping any dry ingredients first.

Fat bombs

Fat bombs need a fat base that will firm up and solidify. This ensures they keep their shape in the fridge and when served at room temperature. They are usually made from a high-fat base of cream cheese, nut butter, butter, ghee, dairy, or coconut cream or coconut oil. This last is particularly beneficial as it contains a type of fat called medium chain triglycerides, which the body absorbs quickly to use as fuel. Dry flavorings of choice can be added to the base fats and the mixture blended before being rolled into balls or molded and coated, then chilled or frozen.

Energy balls

All the energy ball recipes include a mixture of wet and dry ingredients. This not only helps them bind and hold together but also provides a good balance of high protein, healthy fats, and low carbohydrates. You can then add optional extras to provide flavor or nutritional benefits.

The base of dry ingredients could include oats, ground-up nuts and seeds, or protein powder. If you are gluten free, substitute gluten-free oats for oats or use an alternative such as quinoa, millet, or buckwheat flakes.

The wet, sticky ingredients are what will hold it all together. Choose from nut butters, grated or puréed fruit and vegetables, cooked beans, melted coconut oil, or cacao butter or, very occasionally, a drop of yacon syrup or fruit concentrate. You can also use yogurt, coconut cream, cream cheese, and almond milk or other milk alternatives.

The sweeteners

You can use any of the natural, keto-friendly sweeteners listed on page 27, but we like to use liquid stevia. Add just a few drops at a time and adjust to the sweetness you prefer.

ENERGY BOMB FLAVORINGS

The coatings
You don't have to coat energy bombs but the sweet ones look attractive rolled in cocoa powder, chocolate chips, finely chopped nuts, dried shredded coconut, freeze-dried berry powders, matcha green tea powder, crushed freeze-dried berries, ground cinnamon, and grated lime or lemon zest. And some coatings also add texture and flavor. Alternatively, you can drizzle them with melted dark chocolate or even white chocolate if you'll only be using a very small amount. You can roll savory fat bombs in crumbled crispy bacon, chopped herbs, red pepper flakes, chili powder, sweet or smoked paprika, or cayenne pepper. Here are some suggestions:

• Ground spices such as cinnamon, nutmeg, ginger, and cardamom work well for sweet energy bombs.

• Citrus flavorings, including grated orange, lime, and lemon zest, add a distinctive flavor and refreshing sharpness to sweet energy bombs.

• Berries such as raspberries, strawberries, blackberries, or blueberries provide a satisfying sweet, fruity flavor, especially to cheesecake-style fat bombs.

• Vanilla and almond extracts add depth of flavor to sweet energy bombs.

• Cocoa powder or raw cacao powder (higher in minerals and antioxidants) create a lovely chocolate flavor.

Note: If you want to make your energy bombs chocolatey and rich, melt dark chocolate in the microwave or a heatproof bowl set over a pan of simmering water and stir or beat into the base mixture.

• Herbs and low-carb vegetables are good flavorings for savory energy balls.

• Hot spices, such as red pepper flakes, chili powder, cayenne, and paprika, can be used as a flavoring and for rolling and dusting savory energy bombs.

• Oily fish, such as smoked salmon, tuna, and smoked mackerel, add protein and a strong flavor of the sea to the bites.

• Shellfish, such as crabmeat and shrimp, give texture and flavor to creamy balls.

• Meat, including chicken livers and bacon, is great for making parfait balls, plus you can roll savory fat bombs in crumbled crispy bacon for an attractive and tasty finish.

• Cheeses add fat and protein as well as flavor to savory energy bombs.

HIGH PROTEIN RECIPES

These recipes are the perfect choice for snacking or eating before or after a workout. Some of the sweet bites are slightly higher in fruit, which helps replace stores of glycogen (a type of glucose that fuels tired muscles) after exercising.

MAKES 12

1 lb 2 oz (500g)
   ground beef
   (30% fat)
2 garlic cloves
Pinch dried oregano
3 tbsp grated
   Parmesan cheese
4 oz (120g)
   mozzarella, cut
   into 12 cubes
3 tbsp olive oil
Salt and freshly
   ground black
   pepper

PER BITE:
Calories: 210kcal
Fat: 19g
   (7.2g saturated)
Carbohydrates: 0.2g
Sugars: 0.1g
Protein: 8.7g

CHEESY MINI MEATBALLS

These meatballs make tasty snacks, but you can also eat them for dinner topped with tomato sauce on a bed of cauliflower "rice." They're so versatile – try them drizzled with hot sauce, with a tzatziki dip or mixed with zucchini ribbons. Low in carbs and a great source of protein, ground beef also has the keto seal of approval. Always buy high-quality beef with 30 percent fat.

Stir the beef, garlic, oregano, Parmesan, and some salt and pepper in a bowl until well combined. Cover and chill in the fridge for at least 30 minutes to firm up.

Using your hands, take small amounts of the mixture and form into 12 meatballs, molding each one around a mozzarella cube.

Heat the oil in a large skillet set over a medium heat. Fry the meatballs, turning them occasionally, for about 6 to 8 minutes, or until golden brown all over and cooked right through.

Serve the meatballs hot or cold. Store in an airtight container in the fridge for up to 3 days. They also freeze well.

SHRIMP AND AVOCADO WRAPS

MAKES 6

2 medium ripe
  avocados, peeled,
  pitted, and diced

Grated zest and juice
  of ½ lime

9 oz (250g) peeled
  cooked shrimp

4 tbsp mayonnaise

Handful cilantro
  or basil, finely
  chopped

Hot sauce, e.g.
  sriracha, to taste

6 large eggs

2 tbsp butter

Salt and freshly
  ground black
  pepper

PER BITE:

Calories: 279kcal

Fat: 23.4g
  (5.8g saturated)

Carbohydrates: 0.1g

Sugars: 0.1g

Protein: 13g

To make these practically carb-free wraps, use eggs instead of tortillas. For wafer-thin omelets, use a small non-stick skillet. If you're in a hurry, wrap the shrimp and avocado filling in Little Gem or iceberg lettuce. With their jackpot of vitamins and minerals, avocados are a good source of healthy plant oils, making them keto friendly too. If you don't have shrimp, smoked salmon could also be delicious! (See photo.)

Mix the diced avocado and lime zest and juice in a bowl. Add the shrimp, mayonnaise, and herbs and stir well. Add hot sauce to taste.

In a bowl, beat the eggs with a spoonful of water and some salt and pepper.

Melt a little of the butter in a small non-stick skillet set over a low to medium heat. Add one-sixth of the beaten eggs and tilt the pan to cover the base thinly. When the omelet is set and golden underneath, flip it over and cook the other side. Slide onto a plate and keep warm while you cook the other five omelets in the same way.

Divide the avocado and shrimp mixture between the omelets and roll each one up like a wrap.

HOT SAUSAGE BITES

MAKES 24

Butter, for greasing

1 lb (450g) ground
    pork or sausage

1 cup (225g) full-fat
    cream cheese,
    softened

Few sprigs sage,
    finely chopped

Pinch red pepper
    flakes

1 large egg, beaten

1 cup (100g) grated
    cheddar cheese

1 cup (100g) grated
    Parmesan cheese

1 cup (100g) almond
    flour

1 tsp baking soda

Salt and freshly
    ground black
    pepper

PER BITE:

Calories: 134kcal

Fat: 10.7g
    (4.7g saturated)

Carbohydrates: 1.5g

Sugars: 0.6g

Protein: 6.5g

These yummy sausage bites are great for breakfast or brunch or as a low-carb snack at any time of the day. They're best eaten piping hot, but they are good cold too. Buy a pack of good-quality ground pork or sausage without any fillers or additives. Look for the organic sort, which is preservative- and additive-free.

Preheat the oven to 375°F (190°C). Line a baking sheet with aluminum foil and grease generously with butter.

Mix the pork or sausage and cream cheese in a large mixing bowl. Add the sage, red pepper flakes, egg, grated cheeses, almond flour, and baking soda. Season lightly with salt and pepper and stir until everything is well combined.

Take spoonfuls of the mixture and, using your hands, mold them into approximately 1-inch (2.5cm) balls. Place them on the lined baking sheet.

Bake in the oven for 15 to 20 minutes, turning them halfway through, until appetizingly golden brown and cooked inside.

Store in an airtight container in the fridge for up to 3 days, or freeze for up to 3 months.

MARGHERITA "PIZZA" BITES

MAKES 12

1½ cups (200g)
shredded
mozzarella

1 cup (100g) grated
cheddar cheese

¼ cup (60g) ready-
made Italian
tomato pasta
sauce

12 slices pepperoni

Basil sprigs or
arugula

PER BITE:
Calories: 93kcal
Fat: 7.6g
 (4.5g saturated)
Carbohydrates: 0.4g
Sugars: 0.3g
Protein: 5.7g

These low-carb mini pizzas take minutes to make. Don't worry if you don't have pepperoni – any piquant salami or even spicy chorizo works well. Eat as a snack, an appetizer, or as party canapés. Everybody loves them!

Preheat the oven to 375°F (190°C). Line a baking sheet with parchment paper.

Mix the mozzarella and cheddar together in a bowl. Place 12 small heaps on the baking sheet and flatten them out, leaving a little space in between them.

Bake in the oven for 8 to 10 minutes, or until the cheese has melted and is golden brown and crisp around the edges. Remove from the oven and set aside for a few minutes until firm. You can also store these cheesy bases in an airtight container in the fridge for up to 2 days, then crisp them up under a hot broiler before adding the toppings.

Meanwhile, heat the tomato sauce in a pan. Place a teaspoon of sauce on each cheesy base and top with a slice of pepperoni.

Serve immediately, garnished with fresh basil sprigs or arugula.

CHICKEN LIVER PARFAIT BALLS

MAKES 12

- ½ cup (100g) unsalted butter, softened
- 2 shallots, diced
- 1 garlic clove, crushed
- 1 lb (450g) chicken livers, rinsed and cut into pieces
- 2 tbsp cognac (optional)
- ½ tsp ground nutmeg
- ½ tsp ground ginger
- ¾ cup (75g) chopped walnuts or pistachios
- Salt and freshly ground black pepper

PER BITE:
Calories: 140kcal
Fat: 11.5g (5g saturated)
Carbohydrates: 0.9g
Sugars: 0.9g
Protein: 7.6g

Chicken liver has a milder flavor than other types of liver and is nutrient-dense. It's a great source of protein, folic acid, and iron. Instead of nuts, why not roll the parfait balls in crumbled crispy bacon?

Melt a large knob of the butter in a skillet set over a medium heat and cook the shallots and garlic for 5 minutes, or until soft but not colored. Increase the heat slightly and add the chicken livers. Cook for 3 to 4 minutes, turning occasionally, until browned but still slightly pink in the middle. Season with salt and pepper, remove from the pan and place in a blender.

Add the cognac (if using) to the pan and boil until reduced. Pour over the chicken livers and blitz with the nutmeg and ginger until smooth. Add the remaining butter and blitz to combine.

Transfer to a bowl, cover and chill in the fridge for about 8 hours, or overnight, until set firm.

To make the truffles, use a small ice-cream scoop to scoop the mixture into balls, then roll them in the chopped nuts.

Store in an airtight container in the fridge for up to 3 days.

CAULIFLOWER CHEESE BITES

These crispy croquettes are so quick and easy to make. Any strongly flavored hard cheese works well, especially Parmesan. Cauliflower packs quite a nutritional punch with a jackpot of vitamins, minerals, and dietary fiber.

Broil or dry-fry the bacon in a non-stick skillet for 3 to 5 minutes, or until crispy. Drain on paper towels and crumble into small pieces.

Steam the cauliflower florets over a pan of simmering water for 8 to 10 minutes, or until tender. Transfer to a bowl and mash with a fork. Mix in the garlic, chives, cheese, and mustard.

Stir in most of the egg together with the coconut flour or almond meal and bacon. Mix well and season with salt and pepper. If it's too dry, add the remaining egg.

Divide the mixture into 12 pieces and shape each one into a croquette. Roll in the almond flour, shaking off any excess, and place the croquettes on a tray lined with parchment paper. Chill in the fridge for 30 minutes to firm up.

Heat the oil in a large non-stick skillet and cook the croquettes for 2 to 3 minutes each side, or until crispy and golden. Serve immediately.

MAKES 12

- 4 slices bacon
- 1 lb (450g) cauliflower florets
- 2 garlic cloves, crushed
- Few chives, chopped
- 1½ cups (150g) grated cheddar cheese
- 1 tsp Dijon mustard
- 1 large egg, beaten
- 3 tbsp coconut flour or almond meal
- ½ cup (40g) almond flour
- 3 tbsp olive oil
- Salt and freshly ground black pepper

PER BITE:

Calories: 124kcal
Fat: 9.8g
   (3.6g saturated)
Carbohydrates: 2g
Sugars: 0.9g
Protein: 5.9g

CHILI TUNA AND AVOCADO BITES

Crisp and golden, these tuna bites are very "moreish," especially when served piping hot. The creamy avocado complements the flaky tuna and the heat of the chili. Chilies are one of the healthiest foods you can eat. They contain vitamin C and antioxidants, which play an important role in protecting cells and preventing heart disease.

Flake the tuna with a fork and mix with the mayonnaise. Stir in the scallions, red pepper flakes, and Parmesan, then gently fold in the avocado.

Divide the mixture into 15 pieces and, using your hands, mold each one into a ball. Roll in the almond meal to lightly cover all over.

Heat the olive oil in a large skillet set over a medium to high heat. Cook the tuna balls, turning occasionally, for 4 to 5 minutes until crisp and golden brown all over. Serve the balls hot, lukewarm, or cold.

MAKES 15

10½ oz (300g) canned tuna in spring water, drained

5 tbsp mayonnaise

4 scallions, diced

Pinch red pepper flakes

¼ cup (25g) grated Parmesan cheese

1 ripe avocado, peeled, pitted, and diced

½ cup (50g) almond meal

4 tbsp olive oil

PER BITE:

Calories: 115kcal

Fat: 9.1g
  (1.4g saturated)

Carbohydrates: 0.5g

Sugars: 0.3g

Protein: 7g

GOAT'S CHEESE, ROSEMARY, AND RED ONION MUFFINS

MAKES 12

2 tbsp olive oil

2 large red onions, thinly sliced

1 cup (125g) diced goat's cheese

1 tsp finely chopped rosemary

12 large eggs

½ cup (120ml) heavy cream

Scant ½ cup (100ml) water

Salt and freshly ground black pepper

PER BITE:
Calories: 168kcal
Fat: 13.4g
   (6.4g saturated)
Carbohydrates: 2.8g
Sugars: 1.2g
Protein: 9.4g

These flourless muffins are great for breakfast on the go or as a tasty snack at any time of the day. You can add different flavorings – diced chorizo or ham, spinach, fried chopped mushrooms, or red pepper – along with grated cheddar or crumbled feta. As well as being a good source of protein, eggs are rich in vitamins B and D, selenium, zinc, and iron.

Preheat the oven to 350°F (180°C). Line a 12-cup muffin pan.

Heat the oil in a skillet over a low to medium heat and cook the red onion, stirring occasionally, for 6 to 8 minutes until really soft. Mix in the goat's cheese and rosemary and divide between the muffin cups.

Beat the eggs, cream, and water together in a bowl and season lightly with salt and pepper. Pour over the onion mixture in the muffin cups.

Bake in the oven for 25 minutes or until the muffins are set and golden brown.

MATCHA PROTEIN BITES

Cacao butter gives these green nuggets a creamy texture and rich flavor, while the protein powder keeps them grain free, which is perfect if you are following a paleo or gluten free diet. Matcha green tea has very high antioxidant levels (nearly 10 times stronger than green tea). Its stimulant and metabolism-boosting properties are ideal for optimal performance as well as for recovery.

MAKES 20

½ oz (15g) granulated stevia or 1 oz (30g) xylitol/erythritol

½ cup (115g) macadamia nut butter or cashew nut butter

1 tbsp matcha green tea powder

Pinch sea salt

1 tbsp vanilla extract

¼ cup (60g) cacao butter, melted

2–3 oz (60–80g) chocolate or vanilla protein powder

Matcha green tea powder and/or protein powder, to coat

Place the stevia or xylitol in a blender or food processor and grind until very fine.

Add the nut butter, matcha powder, sea salt, vanilla, and melted cacao butter to the food processor and combine.

Add the protein powder and process to form a dough. If the mixture is too soft, add another spoonful of protein powder. Chill the dough in the fridge for 15 to 20 minutes to firm up slightly. Take small spoonfuls of the mixture and roll into walnut-size balls.

Place a little matcha green tea powder and/or protein powder on a plate. Roll the balls in the mixture to coat. Keep in the fridge until required.

PER BITE:

Calories: 81kcal

Fat: 6.2g (0.5g saturated)

Carbohydrates: 1.3g

Sugars: 1g

Protein: 4.4g

BERRY BLISS FITNESS BITES

MAKES 20

- ½ cup (90g) sunflower seeds
- ¼ cup (30g) pumpkin seeds
- ¼ cup (30g) flaxseeds
- 2 oz (60g) vanilla protein powder or collagen powder
- ¼ cup (40g) tahini or nut butter
- 1 tsp granulated stevia
- Juice and zest of 1 lemon
- ¼ cup (30g) dried berries (cherries, cranberries or raisins work well)
- 1 tbsp acai berry powder or other berry superfood powder, to coat (optional)

PER BITE:
Calories: 77kcal
Fat: 5.1g
(0.6g saturated)
Carbohydrates: 3.2g
Sugars: 1.2g
Protein: 3.8g

These delicious bliss balls are perfect for a post-workout treat. The berries provide plenty of antioxidants, which have been shown to reduce muscle soreness and speed up recovery after a hard workout. The combination of protein and carbs is ideal for replenishing stored glycogen, which can be depleted after training, and the protein supports muscle repair.

Place the seeds in a food processor and process until fine. Add the remaining ingredients except for the dried berries and acai berry powder, and process to combine. Add the berries and pulse to break them up but still keep some texture. Add a little water if needed to form a soft dough.

Take walnut-size pieces of the dough and roll into balls. Dust in a little acai berry powder if desired. Store in the fridge for up to 1 week.

(VE) (GF)

PALEO BLUEBERRY MUFFIN BITES

These berry bites are packed with protein and the coconut flour makes them gluten free and suitable for those on a paleo diet. Coconut flour is also higher in fiber and low in carbs, meaning it won't spike your blood sugar levels like grains do – so these bites are ideal for a pre-workout snack to keep energy levels high during training. Coconut flour also contains medium-chain triglycerides, which the body can preferentially use as a fuel too – perfect for boosting your performance.

Place the coconut flour, protein powder, sea salt, stevia, and cinnamon in a mixing bowl or food processor. Combine well. Add the blueberries and tahini, and then add enough milk to form a stiff dough. Do not overprocess the mixture.

Form the mixture into bite-size balls, then refrigerate for at least 30 minutes to firm.

Eat immediately, or store in the fridge for up to 1 week. Alternatively, you can freeze them for up to 3 months.

MAKES 16

½ cup (60g) coconut flour

1 oz (30g) protein powder (vanilla or berry flavor)

Pinch sea salt

1 tsp granulated stevia

½ tsp ground cinnamon

¼ cup (50g) dried blueberries

1 tbsp tahini

½ cup (100ml) coconut milk or almond milk

PER BITE:

Calories: 44kcal

Fat: 1.5g
(0.6g saturated)

Carbohydrates: 4.5g

Sugars: 2.3g

Protein: 2.4g

STRAWBERRY CREAM PROTEIN BITES

MAKES 24

3 oz (90g) colostrum powder or vanilla protein powder

¾ cup (65g) dried shredded coconut

1 tbsp flaxseed meal

¼ cup (50g) cashew nut butter

½ cup (75g) coconut oil, softened

1 oz (30g) xylitol or erythritol

1 tsp vanilla extract

1 cup (120g) frozen strawberries

Pinch sea salt

Colostrum powder or dried shredded coconut, to coat

Naturally creamy thanks to the addition of colostrum or vanilla protein powder, this is an ideal after-workout snack, rich in both protein and carbohydrates. Using strawberries adds plenty of vitamin C and antioxidants, which are perfect for speeding up recovery after exercise. The flaxseed adds fiber and supports digestive health, and together with the protein keeps blood sugar levels balanced.

Place the colostrum, coconut, and flaxseed in a food processor and process until smooth. Add the nut butter, coconut oil (softened, not melted), xylitol, and vanilla and process to combine.

Add the frozen strawberries and a pinch of salt and process until the mixture comes together.

Take small pieces of the mixture and roll into small balls. Roll the balls in a little shredded coconut or colostrum powder.

Store in the fridge until required. These will keep in the fridge for 4–5 days. Alternatively, you can freeze them for up to 3 months.

(VE) (GF)

KALE AND APPLE SUPERGREEN BITES

These green nuggets are rich and creamy, and no one would guess you've added kale! The addition of raw cacao gives them a wonderfully indulgent texture. Low levels of magnesium are known to lead to reduced physical performance, muscle cramps, and soreness after workouts, so the greens here provide plenty of magnesium to support energy production and recovery.

Place all the ingredients in a food processor and blend to form a soft dough.

Take small walnut-size pieces of the mixture and roll into balls. Roll in wheatgrass powder or crushed nuts.

These bites can be frozen for up to 3 months if desired. Once defrosted, they will keep in the fridge for up to 1 week.

MAKES 28

- 1 cup (100g) almond meal
- ½ cup (50g) dried shredded coconut
- Handful kale leaves
- ½ cup (60g) dried apple or pear pieces
- ¼ cup (50g) raw cacao butter, melted
- 2 tsp wheatgrass powder or other supergreens powder
- 2 oz (60g) vanilla protein powder
- 2 tbsp almond milk or coconut cream
- Wheatgrass powder or finely chopped pistachio nuts, to coat

PER BITE:
Calories: 65kcal
Fat: 5g
    (1.1g saturated)
Carbohydrates: 1.7g
Sugars: 1.5g
Protein: 2.9g

ORANGE GOJI ENERGY BITES

MAKES 24

¼ cup (30g) dried shredded coconut

½ cup (60g) almond meal

Pinch sea salt

¼ cup (65g) cashew nut or peanut butter

2 satsumas, peeled

3 cups (50g) puffed brown rice cereal (unsweetened)

1 oz (30g) goji berries

PER BITE:

Calories: 50kcal

Fat: 2.5g
    (0.9g saturated)

Carbohydrates: 3.4g

Sugars: 1.4g

Protein: 3.1g

These deliciously fruity bites make a tasty pick-me-up. Using the whole fruit in the mix means you include all the valuable fiber, which helps balance blood sugar and keeps you feeling fuller for longer. Goji berries are an excellent source of vitamin C and antioxidants.

Place the coconut, ground almonds, salt, nut butter, and satsumas in a food processor and process until the mixture comes together.

Add the rice cereal and goji berries and continue to process until the mixture comes together but there is still texture – do not overprocess.

Take spoonfuls of the mixture and roll into balls. Place on a tray or plate. Refrigerate until needed. These will keep in the fridge for 1 week.

HAZELNUT AND CHOCOLATE BITES

MAKES 22

1 cup (125g)
  hazelnuts

½ cup (50g) raw
  cacao powder

2 oz (50g) erythritol
  or xylitol

½ cup (120g)
  hazelnut butter or
  other nut butter

¼ cup (70g)
  coconut cream
  (see page 118 for
  instructions)

Chopped toasted
  hazelnuts, to coat

PER BITE:
Calories: 104kcal
Fat: 7.8g
    (1.8g saturated)
Carbohydrates: 4.6g
Sugars: 0.6g
Protein: 3g

Wonderfully rich, these bites are packed with protein thanks to the addition of nuts and nut butter. Using coconut cream gives these bites a creamy texture and helps to keep you feeling satisfied by stabilizing blood sugar levels.

Place the hazelnuts, cacao powder, and erythritol in a food processor and process until the hazelnuts are very fine. Add the nut butter and coconut cream, and process to form a soft dough.

Take spoonfuls of the mixture and roll into balls. Place the toasted hazelnuts on a plate and roll the balls in them to coat.

Decorate a tray of bites for a moreish and indulgent dessert for parties. They will also keep in the fridge for up to 1 week.

PLUM CRUMBLE BITES

MAKES 22

1 medium plum,
  stoned, about 2½
  oz (70g)
½ cup (100g)
  almond butter or
  other nut butter
1 tsp vanilla extract
1 tsp granulated
  stevia
2 oz (50g) vanilla
  protein powder
½ cup (40g) almond
  meal
¼ cup (30g) rolled
  oats, quinoa flakes,
  or buckwheat
  flakes
1 tsp ground
  cinnamon
¼ cup (30g) granola
  or additional rolled
  oats

PER BITE:
Calories: 62kcal
Fat: 3.8g
  (0.5g saturated)
Carbohydrates: 2.7g
Sugars: 0.7g
Protein: 3.9g

These light, crunchy bites combine all the ingredients of a fruit crumble in one mouthful. Using fresh plums rather than dried fruit keeps the sugar content low but adds plenty of fiber to support digestive health. The addition of protein powder makes these bites ideal for stabilizing blood sugar levels, preventing dips in energy through the day.

Place the plum, nut butter, vanilla, and stevia in a food processor and blend to form a thick paste. Add the protein powder, almonds, oats, and cinnamon and process again to combine.

Pulse in the granola or oats to combine but leave some crumbly texture.

Scoop the mixture out with a teaspoon and roll into balls.

Store in the fridge for up to 1 week or freeze for up to 3 months. You can eat the bites straight from the freezer or place in the fridge to defrost.

(VE) (GF)

MINT CHOC CHIP CHLORELLA BITES

These are a healthy version of chocolate chip cookie dough. The green superfood powder is optional but gives the little bites a lovely green color as well as being incredibly nutrient rich, containing B vitamins, iron, magnesium, and antioxidants.

Place the cashew nuts, coconut flour, chlorella, protein powder or cacao powder, and stevia in a food processor and process until fine.

Add the nut butter, syrup, and peppermint extract to taste. Process until the mixture begins to form a soft dough. Add in the chocolate chips and almond milk and process until the mixture comes together.

Take small pieces of the dough and roll into balls. Place in the fridge to harden for about 30 minutes. Eat within 1–2 weeks.

MAKES 32

- ¾ cup (125g) cashew nuts
- ¼ cup (30g) coconut flour
- 1 tbsp chlorella powder or other supergreens powder
- 1 oz (30g) chocolate protein powder or raw cacao powder
- ½ oz (15g) granulated stevia, or to taste
- ½ cup (160g) almond nut butter or peanut butter
- ¼ cup (40g) yacon syrup, rice malt syrup, or honey
- ½ tsp peppermint extract
- ½ cup (60g) dark chocolate chips
- 2 tbsp almond milk

PER BITE:

Calories: 77kcal

Fat: 5.3g
    (1.3g saturated)

Carbohydrates: 3.2g

Sugars: 1.1g

Protein: 3.4g

KETO RECIPES

These recipes are low in carbs, high in flavor, and can be prepared in a matter of minutes – and they all come with a keto twist. There's no end to the bite-size cheese balls, melts, fat bombs, popsicles, truffles and mousses you can make with a keto diet in mind.

SPINACH MOZZARELLA BALLS

MAKES 20

7 oz (200g) fresh spinach leaves, washed and trimmed

2 garlic cloves, crushed

3 large eggs, beaten

Pinch grated nutmeg

¾ cup (100g) grated mozzarella

2 tbsp grated Parmesan cheese

1¼ cups (125g) almond flour or almond meal

Salt and freshly ground black pepper

PER BITE:

Calories: 70kcal
Fat: 6g
** (1.4g saturated)**
Carbohydrates: 0.5g
Sugars: 0.3g
Protein: 4g

These cheesy bites make a great snack, but they are also great served with roasted or grilled chicken and meat. If you don't have fresh spinach, you could use frozen instead. Mozzarella is lower in fat than most hard cheeses and is a good source of vitamins and minerals, especially vitamin B12 and calcium.

Preheat the oven to 375°F (190°C). Line a large baking sheet with parchment paper.

Put the wet spinach leaves in a saucepan and cover with a lid. Cook for 2 to 3 minutes over a medium heat, shaking the pan occasionally, until the spinach wilts. Drain in a colander, pressing down with a saucer, then chop finely.

Mix the spinach in a bowl with the garlic, beaten eggs, nutmeg, grated cheeses, and almond flour or almond meal. Season lightly with salt and pepper. The mixture should stick together and be moist and firm enough to mold into balls.

Take spoonfuls of the mixture and roll each one into a ball. Place on the lined baking sheet, leaving a little space in between.

Bake in the oven for 15 to 20 minutes, or until firm and golden brown. Serve hot.

SMOKED MACKEREL AND HORSERADISH TRUFFLES

MAKES 20

9 oz (250g) smoked
 mackerel fillets,
 skinned

¾ cup (200g) full-
 fat cream cheese

3 tbsp butter, at
 room temperature

Grated zest of
 1 lemon

1 tbsp lemon juice

2 tbsp cream
 horseradish

4 scallions, finely
 chopped

2 tbsp capers,
 drained and finely
 chopped

Paprika, for dusting

PER BITE:

Calories: 83kcal

Fat: 7.4g
 (2.8g saturated)

Carbohydrates: 0.8g

Sugars: 0.7g

Protein: 3.3g

These fishy truffles are not only quick and easy to make, but they're healthy too. Smoked mackerel is one of the best sources of heart-friendly omega-3 fats, which also help reduce joint pain and stiffness. You can substitute diced smoked salmon for the mackerel and use lime instead of lemon. If you're serving the truffles straight away, try rolling them in some chopped dill or chives.

Flake the smoked mackerel fillets with a fork and blitz in a food processor or blender with the cream cheese, butter, lemon zest and juice, and cream horseradish.

Transfer to a bowl, and mix in the scallions and capers. Cover and chill in the fridge for about 1 hour to firm up the mixture.

Divide into 20 pieces and, using your hands, mold each one into a ball.

Dust with paprika and store in an airtight container in the fridge for up to 1 week. You can freeze them for up to 3 months.

(GF)

JALAPEÑO POPPERS

You'll like these spicy cream cheese balls because, unlike most jalapeño poppers, you don't have to bake them. Just blitz all the ingredients together, shape into balls, and pop them in the fridge to set – it's so easy!

Set a non-stick skillet over a medium to high heat and, when it's hot, add the bacon. Cook for 3 to 4 minutes, turning once, until golden brown and crispy, then drain on paper towels and crumble into small pieces. Keep the fat that's run out of the bacon.

Blitz the cream cheese, butter, grated cheese, and any leftover bacon fat in a blender or food processor until well combined. Stir in the chili, garlic, and parsley.

Transfer to a bowl, cover, and chill in the fridge for 1 hour or until firm.

Divide the mixture into 12 pieces. Using your hands, form each one into a ball and roll in the crumbled bacon. Eat immediately or store in an airtight container in the fridge for up to 3 days.

MAKES 12

6 slices bacon

½ cup (100g) full-fat cream cheese

3 tbsp unsalted butter, softened

½ cup (50g) grated cheddar or Monterey Jack cheese

2 jalapeño chilies, deseeded and diced

1 garlic clove, crushed

1 tbsp finely chopped parsley

PER BITE:

Calories: 97kcal

Fat: 9.2g (5.2g saturated)

Carbohydrates: 0.5g

Sugars: 0.4g

Protein: 2.9g

CHEESE BALLS WITH BACON AND SWEET CHILI

MAKES 24

1 cup (250g) full-fat cream cheese

½ cup (50g) grated mozzarella

2 tbsp mango chutney

1 tsp curry powder

2 scallions, diced

Few cilantro sprigs, finely chopped

9 oz (250g) bacon

Sweet chili sauce, for drizzling (optional)

PER BITE:
Calories: 49kcal
Fat: 4.5g
   (2.5g saturated)
Carbohydrates: 1.2g
Sugars: 1.1g
Protein: 2g

Keep a container of these cream cheese balls handy in the fridge for when you feel like a nutritious bite. If you love hot and spicy food, add some diced chili, or why not stir in some chopped smoked salmon and dill, flaked tuna, or white crabmeat? Like other fat bombs, they're very versatile.

Mix the cream cheese, mozzarella, mango chutney, curry powder, scallions, and cilantro in a bowl until well combined. Cover and chill in the fridge for 1 hour to firm up.

Broil or dry-fry the bacon in a non-stick skillet until golden brown and crispy. Drain on paper towels and crumble into small pieces.

Roll tablespoons of the cream cheese mixture into small balls, and then roll them in the bacon pieces. Serve, if desired, drizzled with sweet chili sauce. Store in the fridge for 2 to 3 days.

PROSCIUTTO, PEPPER, AND CHEESE MELTS

These truffles are made with delicious goat's cheese, roasted peppers, and prosciutto. There is a great contrast between the soft, creamy filling and the crispy exterior. You can eat them hot or cold – they're great either way.

Put the goat's cheese in a mixing bowl and mash with a fork. Add the cream cheese, peppers, chives, garlic salt, and red pepper flakes and mix well.

Divide into 12 portions and, using your hands, shape each one into a ball. Arrange the balls on a baking sheet lined with parchment paper, then cover and freeze for about 20 minutes.

Wrap each ball in a slice of prosciutto, winding the ham around to enclose the cheese.

Place a large skillet over a medium heat and, when it's hot, add the cheese balls. Cook for 3 to 4 minutes, turning occasionally, until golden brown and crispy all over.

Serve hot, drizzled with balsamic vinegar if using, or leave to cool and store in an airtight container in the fridge for up to 5 days.

MAKES 12

- 3½ oz (100g) soft goat's cheese
- ¾ cup (200g) full-fat cream cheese
- 2½ oz (75g) bottled roasted peppers, drained and diced
- Small bunch chives, chopped
- Pinch garlic salt
- Pinch red pepper flakes
- 4½ oz (125g) wafer-thin prosciutto (approx. 12 slices)
- Balsamic vinegar, for drizzling (optional)

PER BITE:
Calories: 90kcal
Fat: 7.4g
   (4.5g saturated)
Carbohydrates: 1g
Sugars: 0.9g
Protein: 4.9g

REALLY GREEN AVOCADO COCONUT BITES

MAKES 16

½ cup (150g) coconut butter (at room temperature)

1 oz (30g) protein powder

¼ cup (30g) almond flour or almond meal

2 tbsp coconut sugar

1 cup (50g) shredded raw spinach or kale

1 large ripe avocado, peeled, pitted, and cubed

A few drops vanilla extract (optional)

¼ cup (50g) finely chopped toasted almonds

PER BITE:

Calories: 131kcal

Fat: 10.6g
(6.1g saturated)

Carbohydrates: 4.6g

Sugars: 2.3g

Protein: 3.7g

These delicious bites are so appealing with their exquisite lime green color. Better still, they are very healthy and packed with protein, vitamins, and minerals. They are rolled in toasted almonds, but you could substitute other chopped nuts, coconut flakes (see photo), cacao nibs, ground almonds, cocoa powder, or even melted dark chocolate.

Put the coconut butter, protein powder, almond flour, coconut sugar, spinach or kale, avocado, and the vanilla extract (if using) in a blender or food processor.

Blitz until you have a really smooth paste. You may have to keep stopping and scraping down the sides of the blender until everything is well combined.

Transfer to a sealed container and place in the freezer for at least 30 minutes, or until the mixture is chilled and firm.

Divide the mixture into 16 pieces and roll each one into a ball. Roll the balls in the chopped almonds and serve. These bites will keep well stored in an airtight container in the fridge for up to 1 week, or they can be frozen for up to 3 months.

VANILLA CHEESECAKE FAT BOMBS

MAKES 12

1 cup (250g) full-fat
cream cheese

½ cup (125g)
butter, at room
temperature

½ cup (120ml)
heavy cream

2 tsp vanilla extract

Grated zest of
1 orange

Liquid sweetener, to
taste (approx.
7–10 drops)

Grated white or dark
chocolate, for
sprinkling

PER BITE:

Calories: 185kcal

Fat: 18g
(12g saturated)

Carbohydrates: 2.3g

Sugars: 2.3g

Protein: 1.4g

It takes less than 10 minutes to make a batch of fat bombs. I've used some orange zest for extra flavor, but you could try lemon zest or just stick with the vanilla. It's a good idea to invest in a silicone muffin/cupcake pan, as the fat bombs won't stick and will pop out more easily. If you don't have one, freeze the mixture and then scoop out the balls.

Beat the cream cheese and butter until combined and smooth in a food mixer on low speed or using a handheld electric whisk.

Add the cream, vanilla extract, and orange zest, and beat until the mixture is thick and creamy. Sweeten to taste with liquid sweetener, adding a few drops at a time, and beat again.

Use a small ice-cream scoop to shape the mixture into balls and place in a 12-hole muffin pan.

Chill in the fridge for 2 hours until set firm, or pop the pan into the freezer for 30 minutes.

Remove the fat bombs from the pan and sprinkle with grated chocolate. Store in an airtight container in the fridge for up to 2 weeks.

AVOCADO CREAM POPS

These avocado pops are deliciously creamy. If you don't have lime, use lemon – not only for a zingy flavor, but to keep the avocado from discoloring. The pops are dipped in chocolate, which makes them rather decadent. You could sprinkle toasted coconut or chopped pistachios over the chocolate.

MAKES 6

2 ripe avocados, peeled and pitted

1½ cups (360ml) coconut milk

Juice of 1 lime

Granulated sweetener, e.g. stevia, to taste

3½ oz (100g) dark chocolate (minimum 70% cocoa solids)

1 tbsp coconut oil

PER BITE:

Calories: 260kcal

Fat: 18g (13.5g saturated)

Carbohydrates: 8.3g

Sugars: 4g

Protein: 5.7g

Pulse the avocado flesh, coconut milk, and lime juice in a blender or food processor until smooth and creamy. Sweeten to taste.

Divide the mixture into six popsicle molds and insert some wooden sticks. Freeze for at least 6 hours or, better still, overnight until frozen solid.

Line a baking sheet with parchment paper or use a silicone mat. Turn out the popsicles by running the molds under hot water and place the popsicles on the lined tray or mat. Freeze for at least 1 hour until frozen solid.

Break the chocolate into pieces and put them in a heatproof bowl with the coconut oil. Set the bowl over a pan of simmering water until the chocolate melts. Set aside to cool a little.

Dip the ends of the frozen avocado cream pops into the melted chocolate. Place on the lined tray or mat and freeze until set solid.

(VE) (GF)

BERRIES YOGURT POPS

These fruity, creamy ice pops are so cooling and refreshing on a hot day. Make a batch in the summer to keep in the freezer. Everyone loves them, not only children. You can swirl the fruit and yogurt together if you don't want to bother layering them. Try substituting blackberries, raspberries, or pitted cherries for the blueberries – they're all delicious.

Blitz half the berries in a blender or food processor. Sweeten to taste with liquid sweetener, adding a few drops at a time.

Mix the coconut yogurt with the vanilla extract in a bowl.

Swirl the whole and blitzed berries with the yogurt and spoon the mixture into six popsicle molds. Insert some wooden sticks.

Freeze for at least 6 hours, or overnight, until firm and frozen.

To turn out the blueberry yogurt pops, run the molds under hot water for a few seconds – don't let the water get inside the molds.

You can keep these pops frozen for up to 1 month.

MAKES 6

1 cup (200g) fresh or frozen and thawed berries

Liquid sweetener, to taste

1¼ cups (300g) dairy-free coconut yogurt

1 tsp vanilla extract

PER BITE:

Calories: 81kcal

Fat: 5g (5g saturated)

Carbohydrates: 8g

Sugars: 4g

Protein: 0.8g

GRANOLA WITH CHOCOLATE DRIZZLE

MAKES 20

3 tbsp coconut oil

¼ cup (60g) smooth nut butter, e.g. peanut or almond

2 tbsp granulated sweetener, e.g. stevia, to taste

1¼ cups (150g) chopped walnuts

½ cup (100g) chopped blanched almonds

½ cup (75g) mixed seeds, e.g. pumpkin, sunflower, sesame

¼ cup (40g) flaxseed meal

1 cup (60g) unsweetened coconut flakes

1 tsp vanilla extract

1¾ oz (50g) dark chocolate (minimum 70% cocoa solids)

PER BITE:

Calories: 185kcal

Fat: 16.4g
(5g saturated)

Carbohydrates: 2.9g

Sugars: 1.9g

Protein: 5.3g

Low-carb, gluten-free, easy to make … what's not to like about this granola? You can vary the nuts and seeds according to personal taste. Try flavoring it with ground cinnamon or nutmeg instead of vanilla, or adding a spoonful of cacao powder for extra flavor (see photo page 19).

Preheat the oven to 325°F (170°C). Line a large baking sheet with parchment paper.

Heat the coconut oil, nut butter, and sweetener in a pan set over a low heat until the oil and nut butter melt and the sweetener dissolves. Add the nuts, mixed seeds, flaxseed, coconut flakes, and vanilla. Stir until everything is combined.

Spoon onto the lined baking sheet, pressing it down in an even layer. Bake in the oven for 15 to 20 minutes until golden brown. Remove and leave to cool and firm up.

Break the chocolate into pieces and put them in a heatproof bowl. Set the bowl over a pan of simmering water until the chocolate melts. Drizzle over the granola and leave until set.

Break the granola into pieces or clusters and store in a sealed container in a cool place. It will stay fresh for up to 1 week.

(GF)

STRAWBERRIES AND CREAM FROZEN BITES

Keep a container of these little creamy bites in the freezer for snacking on whenever you feel in need of a cooling pick-me-up. You can substitute raspberries or blackberries for the strawberries.

Beat the cream cheese and butter until light and fluffy in a food mixer or with a handheld electric whisk.

Add the coconut oil, vanilla, and strawberries and beat until well combined. Add liquid sweetener to taste.

Spoon the mixture into silicone cupcake molds and freeze for at least 3 hours or overnight.

Break the chocolate into pieces and put them in a heatproof bowl. Set the bowl over a pan of simmering water until the chocolate melts.

Remove the frozen bites from the molds and place on a baking sheet lined with parchment paper or a silicone mat. Drizzle with melted chocolate and replace in the freezer for at least 30 minutes until set solid.

Remove from the freezer about 10 minutes or so before eating them, so they soften a little. Store in an airtight container in the freezer for up to 1 month.

MAKES 24

1 cup (225g) full-fat cream cheese, softened

¼ cup (75g) butter, softened

2 tbsp coconut oil

1 tsp vanilla extract

14 oz (400g) fresh strawberries, hulled and chopped

Liquid sweetener, e.g. stevia, to taste

1¾ oz (50g) white chocolate, for drizzling

PER BITE:

Calories: 73kcal

Fat: 6.6g
(4.5g saturated)

Carbohydrates: 2.5g

Sugars: 2.5g

Protein: 1.2g

CHOCOLATE GANACHE TRUFFLES

MAKES 20

1 cup (175g) dark chocolate chips

2 tbsp coconut oil

½ cup (120ml) heavy cream

1 tbsp vanilla extract

Pinch sea salt

1 tsp liquid sweetener, e.g. stevia (or to taste)

3 tbsp cocoa powder

½ cup (40g) dried shredded coconut

PER BITE:

Calories: 111kcal

Fat: 9.5g
(6.4g saturated)

Carbohydrates: 3.4g

Sugars: 2.7g

Protein: 1.1g

These truffles are so yummy. Enjoy them as an energy snack, a dessert, or just as a treat. As well as tasting great, they're good for you. Dark chocolate is choc-full of antioxidants and is good for heart health. Roll in cocoa and/or coconut (see photo page 29).

Put the chocolate and coconut oil in a heatproof bowl and set the bowl over a pan of simmering water until the chocolate melts.

Gently stir in the cream, vanilla, and sea salt, plus sweetener to taste.

Cover and chill in the fridge for at least 30 minutes to firm and set, or pop into the freezer for 20 to 30 minutes.

Use a small ice-cream or cookie scoop to scoop out the mixture and, using your hands, roll into balls. Roll half of them in the cocoa powder and the rest in the coconut.

You can store the truffles in an airtight container lined with parchment paper in the fridge for up to 3 days.

(GF)

LEMON AND POPPY SEED CHEESECAKE TRUFFLES

You can serve these delicious cheesecake bites as a dessert. The poppy seeds add texture and flavor and are a rich source of healthy fat, protein, and essential minerals, especially calcium and iron. You can also swap the seeds for a handful of freeze-dried raspberries and add to the coconut for coating.

MAKES 20

1 cup (225g) full-fat cream cheese

1¼ cups (120g) dried shredded coconut

Grated zest of 1 lemon

Juice of ½ lemon

Artificial sweetener, to taste

1 tbsp poppy seeds

COATING:

1¾ oz (50g) dark chocolate (minimum 70% cocoa solids)

1 cup (100g) dried shredded coconut

PER BITE:

Calories: 108kcal

Fat: 9.9g (4.8g saturated)

Carbohydrates: 2.5g

Sugars: 2.4g

Protein: 1.4g

Line a baking sheet with parchment paper.

Blitz the cream cheese, coconut, zest, and juice in a food processor until smooth. Add sweetener to taste and blitz again. Add the seeds and pulse until they are distributed through the mixture.

Divide the mixture into 20 pieces and, using your hands, mold them into balls. Arrange on the lined baking sheet and chill in the fridge or place in the freezer for at least 1 hour until firm.

Break the chocolate into pieces and put them in a heatproof bowl. Set the bowl over a pan of simmering water until the chocolate melts.

Roll the balls in the coconut, drizzle with the chocolate, and chill until set. Store in a sealed container lined with parchment paper in the fridge for up to 1 week or freeze for 1 month.

RED VELVET CHOCOLATE MACADAMIA BITES

These little bites (see photo pages 94–95) make a great bedtime snack – the cherries boost your melatonin levels, regulate your sleep cycle, and relieve insomnia, while the high magnesium content of the dark chocolate steadies your heart rhythm and aids restful sleep.

Blitz the cherries, beets, and coconut cream in a blender until smooth.

Break the chocolate into pieces and melt in a heatproof bowl suspended over a pan of simmering water. Remove from the heat and stir in the cherry and beets mixture until well combined and smooth.

Cover and chill in the fridge for 4 hours until firm and set. Alternatively, freeze for 1 hour.

Using your hands, mold the mixture into 16 small balls. Roll them in the chopped nuts and freeze-dried berries and place on a baking sheet lined with parchment paper.

Chill in the fridge for 1 hour or pop them in the freezer until set hard. Store in an airtight container in the fridge for up to 1 week, or for 3 months in the freezer.

MAKES 16

- ½ cup (75g) red cherries, pitted
- 2½ oz (75g) cooked beets (note: not beets in vinegar)
- ¼ cup (75g) coconut cream
- 5 oz (150g) dark chocolate (minimum 70% cocoa solids)
- ½ cup (75g) finely chopped macadamia nuts
- 2 tbsp crushed freeze-dried berries

PER BITE:

Calories: 101kcal

Fat: 8.3g
   (3.7g saturated)

Carbohydrates: 4.3g

Sugars: 3.6g

Protein: 1.5g

TOASTED ALMOND SNOWBALLS

MAKES 20

¾ cup (120g) butter

1 large egg, beaten

½ tsp almond extract

¾ cup (125g) toasted whole almonds

½ cup (60g) coconut flour

4½ oz (125g) sugar-free powdered sugar

Rose water, for spraying

PER BITE:
Calories: 108kcal
Fat: 8.7g
  (3.8g saturated)
Carbohydrates: 3.5g
Sugars: 0.8g
Protein: 2.6g

These little almond bites are made with homemade sugar-free powdered "sugar." Just pulse 3½ oz (100g) granulated sweetener (e.g. Splenda, stevia, or xylitol) with 1 tsp cornstarch in a blender or coffee grinder until you have a fine powder.

Preheat the oven to 325°F (170°C). Line a baking sheet with parchment paper.

Melt the butter in a pan set over a low heat. Pour into a bowl and mix with the beaten egg and almond extract.

Blitz the almonds in a food processor until finely ground. Mix with the coconut flour and 6½ tablespoons of the powdered sugar, and beat into the butter and egg mixture until you have a smooth dough. If it's too moist, add more coconut flour.

Divide the dough into 20 pieces and, using your hands, roll each one into a ball. Place on the lined baking sheet and bake in the oven for 25 to 30 minutes until firm and lightly browned.

Spray lightly with rose water, then dust with the remaining powdered sugar and cool. Store in an airtight container for up to 5 days.

PEANUT BUTTER BITES

These creamy peanut bites are something special. They are a great on-the-go snack and give an instant energy boost whenever you're feeling weary. They are sugar-free, but a tablespoon of maple syrup (instead of sweetener) adds a lovely hint of caramel.

Put the peanut butter, cacao butter, coconut oil, vanilla extract, and salt in a heatproof glass bowl. Set it over a pan of simmering water for 4 to 5 minutes until it melts, stirring occasionally.

Sweeten to taste with the liquid sweetener, adding a few drops at a time.

Divide the mixture into 12 individual silicone muffin molds or a mini muffin pan lined with cases. Sprinkle with a little sea salt.

Freeze for 1 hour until set and totally solid. Remove from the molds or muffin pan and transfer to a sealed container or freezer bag. Store in the freezer for up to 1 month.

MAKES 12

½ cup (125g) smooth unsweetened peanut butter

¼ cup (60g) raw cacao butter

¼ cup (60g) coconut oil

1 tsp vanilla extract

Pinch sea salt flakes, plus extra for sprinkling

Liquid sweetener, e.g. stevia, to taste (approx. 5–10 drops)

PER BITE:

Calories: 154kcal

Fat: 16.8g (8g saturated)

Carbohydrates: 1.2g

Sugars: 0.5g

Protein: 3.3g

NUTTY CHILI CHOCOLATE BARK

MAKES 20

Olive oil spray

9 oz (250g) dark chocolate (minimum 70% cocoa solids)

1 tsp vanilla extract

½ oz (15g) freeze-dried blueberries or raspberries

½ cup (75g) chopped pistachios

¾ cup (75g) flaked toasted almonds

½ tsp red pepper flakes

Pinch sea salt flakes

PER BITE:

Calories: 121kcal

Fat: 9g (3.7g saturated)

Carbohydrates: 5g

Sugars: 3g

Protein: 3.4g

This is the easiest way to make chocolate bark – just melt the chocolate and sprinkle with some crunchy toppings. Try using the really bitter chocolate (85 percent cocoa solids), as the freeze-dried berries add a touch of sweetness. You can flavor the melted chocolate with ground spices (cinnamon, ginger, chili, or cayenne) and top with seeds (chia, sesame, sunflower, or pumpkin) and shredded coconut.

Line a baking sheet with parchment paper and spray lightly with oil, or use a non-stick silicone mat.

Break the chocolate into pieces and melt in a heatproof bowl suspended over a pan of simmering water. Stir in the vanilla extract.

Pour the melted chocolate onto the lined baking sheet and spread it out thinly and evenly with a palette knife. Sprinkle the freeze-dried berries, nuts, red pepper flakes, and sea salt over the top.

Chill in the fridge for at least 3 hours until the bark is set solid. Alternatively, chill in the freezer for at least 1 hour. Remove and break roughly into approximately 20 pieces. Store in an airtight container in the fridge for up to 5 days.

NO-BAKE NUTTY BROWNIE BITES

These no-bake brownies are practically carb- and sugar-free, and they're made in minutes. They look pretty rolled in green pistachios, but you could use any chopped nuts, shredded coconut, or even some cocoa. Nuts are a great keto choice as they are a rich source of healthy plant oil and low in carbs.

MAKES 30

1 cup (100g) pecan halves

¾ cup (200g) almond or pistachio butter

½ cup (50g) cocoa powder

1 tsp vanilla extract

½ tsp sea salt flakes

Liquid sweetener, e.g. stevia, to taste

2 tbsp almond flour or almond meal

¼ cup (50g) dark chocolate chips

½ cup (80g) chopped pistachios

PER BITE:
Calories: 98kcal
Fat: 8.2g
   (1.2g saturated)
Carbohydrates: 1.9g
Sugars: 1.3g
Protein: 3.6g

Blitz the pecans in a food processor and then add the nut butter, cocoa, vanilla, and sea salt. Blitz until everything is well combined.

Sweeten to taste, adding a few drops at a time, and then add the almond flour. If the mixture is too moist, add some more flour; if it's too dry and crumbly, add a little milk.

Lastly, add the chocolate chips and blitz briefly. Divide the mixture into 30 pieces and roll each one into a ball.

Roll the balls in the chopped pistachios, pressing them in gently with your fingers. Place on a baking sheet lined with parchment paper, then cover and chill in the fridge for at least 30 minutes until firm, or freeze for about 15 to 20 minutes.

Store in an airtight container in the fridge for up to 3 days.

CITRUS COCONUT TRUFFLES

MAKES 24

1 cup (225g) full-fat cream cheese, softened

4 tbsp coconut oil, melted

½ cup (40g) almond meal

Juice of ½ lemon

2–3 tsp liquid sweetener, e.g. stevia

¾ cup (75g) dried shredded coconut

Grated zest of 1 lemon

PER BITE:

Calories: 74kcal

Fat: 7.3g
(5.2g saturated)

Carbohydrates: 0.7g

Sugars: 0.6g

Protein: 1g

These no-bake, sugar-free truffles are perfect for when you're craving something sweet or want an easy dessert. Try one mid-afternoon with a mug of fresh mint tea when you want an energy boost. For a more intense lemony flavor, add some grated lemon zest to the cream mixture.

Beat the cream cheese and coconut oil until smooth and creamy. It's best to do this in a food processor or with a handheld electric whisk.

Beat in the almond meal and lemon juice. Beat in the liquid sweetener, a teaspoon at a time, until you have the desired sweetness. Finally, add 4 tablespoons of the shredded coconut.

Cover and chill in the refrigerator for at least 30 minutes to firm up.

Mix the remaining coconut with the grated lemon zest in a bowl.

Using your hands, shape the chilled mixture into 24 balls. Roll them in the lemony dried shredded coconut and store in an airtight container in the fridge.

COCONUT AND LIME MINI MOUSSES

MAKES 10

1¼ cups (300ml) heavy cream

1 cup (225g) mascarpone, softened

¼ cup (60ml) coconut milk

Grated zest and juice of 2 limes

Liquid sweetener, e.g. stevia, to taste

3 tbsp toasted shredded or flaked coconut

PER BITE:

Calories: 256kcal

Fat: 26.7g (17.4g saturated)

Carbohydrates: 2.2g

Sugars: 1.4g

Protein: 1.9g

This creamy mousse is really refreshing thanks to the lime zest and juice. If you don't have limes you could substitute lemons or oranges. Mascarpone is an Italian soft cheese, often associated with tiramisu, which is made from cream. It is low in carbs with a very high fat content (about 90 percent of the calories are from fat).

Beat the cream until it's thick and stands in stiff peaks. You can do this in a food mixer or in a bowl with a handheld electric whisk.

In a food mixer, beat the mascarpone with the coconut milk, lime zest, and juice until smooth and creamy. Add liquid sweetener to taste. Add the whipped cream and beat until everything is well combined.

Divide the mixture into 10 small ramekins (custard cups) or silicone molds and chill in the fridge for at least 2–3 hours until the mousse is firm and set. Serve sprinkled with toasted coconut.

The mousse will keep well in the fridge for up to 4 days.

(GF)

CHOCA-MOCHA MASCARPONE MINI MOUSSES

These mini mousses are so easy to make and great for dessert or as a snack. They aren't sweetened as they have a great bitter chocolate and coffee taste, but you could add some liquid sweetener.

Break the chocolate into pieces and place in a heatproof bowl suspended over a pan of simmering water. When the chocolate melts, remove the saucepan from the heat immediately.

Lift the bowl off the pan and gently beat the mascarpone into the melted chocolate. Add the espresso coffee and whisk until smooth.

In a separate bowl, whip the cream until it stands in stiff peaks. Gently fold the whipped cream into the chocolate mascarpone mixture using a figure-eight movement until well combined.

Divide the mixture into 10 small ramekins (custard cups) or silicone molds and chill in the fridge for at least 2–3 hours until the mousse is firm and set. Serve topped with dark chocolate shavings or coffee beans, if desired.

The mousse will keep well in the fridge for up to 3 days.

MAKES 10

4½ oz (125g) dark chocolate (minimum 70% cocoa solids)

½ cup (125g) mascarpone

2 tbsp hot strong espresso coffee

1 cup (250ml) heavy cream, whipped

Dark chocolate shavings or coffee beans, to decorate (optional)

PER BITE:

Calories: 240kcal

Fat: 23g (14.6g saturated)

Carbohydrates: 4.8g

Sugars: 3.8g

Protein: 2.3g

LOW SUGAR
RECIPES

Now for the fun stuff – the bites in this chapter are
alll low in sugar and ideal for sweet cravings or to
have after dinner instead of dessert. Many of them
also make great gifts – simply package in a jar or box
and add ribbon and a label.

RED VELVET BITES

Beets and chocolate are a great combination. Beets contain nitrates, which the body converts to nitric oxide, in turn boosting blood flow and improving oxygenation of the body, allowing you to exercise harder for longer. Dark chocolate is rich in a substance called epicatechin, a nutrient-rich flavonol that also increases nitric oxide production.

Place the beets, fruit, and coconut cream in a blender and purée until smooth. Transfer to a small pan with the chocolate and heat gently, stirring all the time until the chocolate has melted. Pour the mixture into a bowl and chill in the fridge for 3–4 hours or freeze for 1 hour to harden.

Once firm, roll teaspoonfuls of the mixture into small balls with your hands. Roll in berry powder, freeze-dried berries, or cacao powder to coat.

Freeze or place the bites in the fridge to harden. They will keep in the fridge for 1 week or in the freezer for about 3 months.

MAKES 14

2 oz (60g) cooked beets (without vinegar)

2 oz (60g) pitted cherries, raspberries, or strawberries – fresh or frozen

¼ cup (60g) canned coconut cream (see page 118 for instructions)

5½ oz (150g) dark chocolate, broken into pieces

2 tsp acai berry powder

Berry powder, crushed freeze-dried berries or raw cacao, to coat

PER BITE:
Calories: 80kcal
Fat: 5.6g
    (3.8g saturated)
Carbohydrates: 5.9g
Sugars: 1.2g
Protein: 1.5g

CHEWY BANANA BREAD BITES

These are slightly sweet bites with the addition of the banana chips. Buckwheat is a nutritious gluten-free grain, rich in antioxidants such as rutin, which can help strengthen blood vessels and improve circulation. It is also a naturally rich source of protein and fiber to help balance blood sugar and keep you feeling fuller for longer. And it's perfect for energizing the body too, being rich in both B vitamins and magnesium.

Place the banana chips, walnuts, and buckwheat in a food processor and process briefly to break up the chips and nuts.

Add the remaining ingredients and process briefly so the mixture comes together.

Form the mixture into small balls. Keep in the fridge for up to 1 week.

MAKES 24

½ cup (75g) banana chips

½ cup (60g) walnuts

½ cup (75g) dry buckwheat groats, soaked in water for 1 hour then drained

¼ cup (50g) almond nut butter

2 tsp ground cinnamon

Pinch sea salt

2 tsp vanilla extract

2 tsp coconut oil, softened

PER BITE:

Calories: 63kcal

Fat: 4.2g
    (1.5g saturated)

Carbohydrates: 4.6g

Sugars: 1.3g

Protein: 1.4g

APPLE CINNAMON BREAKFAST BITES

MAKES 18

¼ cup (30g) dried apples

1 tsp vanilla extract

1 oz (30g) lucuma powder

½ cup (65g) sunflower seeds

½ apple, peeled

2 tbsp flaxseed meal

2 tsp ground cinnamon

Pinch sea salt

½ cup (50g) rolled oats

Powdered xylitol and cinnamon, to coat

PER BITE:
Calories: 50kcal
Fat: 2.3g
 (0.3g saturated)
Carbohydrates: 5.2g
Sugars: 1.5g
Protein: 1.5g

Fancy an alternative for breakfast? These delicious oat nuggets will energize you in the morning. Crammed with plenty of slow-releasing carbohydrates, fiber, and protein, they make an ideal start to the day. The lucuma gives them a great flavor and sweetness.

Place all the ingredients except the oats, powdered xylitol, and cinnamon in a food processor and blitz to break up the seeds. Add the oats and pulse briefly to bring the mixture together, keeping some texture.

Form into walnut-size balls. Roll each ball in the powdered xylitol and cinnamon mixture.

Store in the fridge for up to 1 week.

(GF)

RASPBERRY LEMON CHEESECAKE BITES

A wonderful alternative to an ice-cream dessert! These creamy frozen nuggets are light and fruity and perfect if you are craving pudding. Freeze-dried berries provide a colorful topping to these bites.

Place the cream cheese, lemon zest, xylitol or stevia, raspberries, and coconut or protein powder in a food processor and blend until smooth. Spoon into a bowl and freeze for 1–2 hours until firm.

Place the coconut and crushed freeze-dried berries on a plate. Take bite-size pieces of the frozen mixture and roll into balls. Roll in the coconut mixture and place on a sheet of parchment paper.

Heat the dark chocolate in a glass bowl set over a pan of simmering water and stir until melted. Use a spoon to drizzle the chocolate over the tops of the balls to decorate.

Place the bites in the freezer until required. Eat straight from the freezer.

MAKES 10

½ cup (100g) cream cheese

Zest of 1 lemon

1 tbsp xylitol or granulated stevia, to taste

1 tbsp freeze-dried raspberries (optional)

½ cup (60g) fresh raspberries

¾ cup (60g) dried shredded coconut or vanilla or berry protein powder

DECORATION:

¼ cup (30g) dried shredded coconut

1 tbsp freeze-dried berries, crushed

2 oz (50g) dark chocolate

PER BITE:

Calories: 108kcal

Fat: 8.6g
(6.6g saturated)

Carbohydrates: 4.9g

Sugars: 0.8g

Protein: 1.9g

APRICOT AND COCONUT BITES

MAKES 15

1 cup (90g) dried shredded coconut

1 tbsp coconut oil

Zest of 1 orange

1 tbsp ground chia seeds

2 fresh pitted apricots (about 3½ oz/100g)

¼ cup (30g) dried shredded coconut or 2 oz (60g) melted dark chocolate, to coat

PER BITE:

Calories: 56kcal

Fat: 4.7g
   (3.8g saturated)

Carbohydrates: 1.2g

Sugars: 0.8g

Protein: 1.4g

This simple recipe uses just a handful of ingredients. Using fresh apricots rather than dried reduces the overall sugar content while still providing natural sweetness and fiber. The chia seeds help to bind the mixture. You can coat these in dried shredded coconut or, for a more indulgent treat, dip in chocolate.

Line a baking sheet with parchment paper. Place all the ingredients in a food processor and process to combine, but keep a little texture in the mixture.

Roll tablespoons of the mixture into balls. You can either roll the balls in the coconut or freeze until firm and then coat in melted chocolate.

Place the bites on the baking sheet and freeze for 1 hour to harden. Store in the fridge for up to 1 week or keep in the freezer.

MANGO AND TURMERIC BITES

MAKES 25

1½ cups (150g) rolled oats

¼ cup (30g) coconut flour

1 tbsp granulated stevia

½ tsp turmeric

½ tsp ground cinnamon

½ cup (130g) mango chunks (roughly half a large mango)

1 tsp vanilla extract

¼ cup (75g) cashew butter or other nut butter

1 tbsp coconut oil

Extra granulated stevia and turmeric, to coat

PER BITE:

Calories: 55kcal

Fat: 2.6g
   (0.8g saturated)

Carbohydrates: 5.4g

Sugars: 0.6g

Protein: 1.8g

Turmeric is a fabulous super spice – known for its anti-inflammatory and antioxidant properties – and combines well with the sweetness of mango. Using oats is a great way to add plenty of soluble fiber, protein, and B vitamins to keep the body energized through the day.

Place all the ingredients in a food processor and blend together to form a soft dough.

Take spoonfuls of the mixture and shape into small balls. Roll the balls in a mixture of granulated stevia and turmeric to coat.

Place in the fridge until required, for up to 1 week. The bites can also be frozen for up to 3 months.

CHOCOLATE AND COCONUT BITES

MAKES 24

½ cup (125g) coconut cream (see note in recipe intro)

2 tbsp yacon syrup, maple syrup, or rice malt syrup

2 tbsp coconut oil

1 cup (100g) dried shredded coconut

Pinch sea salt

1¼ cups (200g) chocolate chips (use sugar-free, dairy-free chocolate if you're vegan)

1 tsp coconut oil

PER BITE:

Calories: 90kcal

Fat: 7.4g
  (5.7g saturated)

Carbohydrates: 4.1g

Sugars: 0.8g

Protein: 1.3g

A delicious mini morsel. For the coconut cream, chill an unopened can of full-fat coconut milk in the fridge for a few hours before using – the cream sets at the top of the can, making it easier to scoop out. Save the rest of the can to use in smoothies.

Place the coconut cream, syrup, and coconut oil in a saucepan over a low heat. Stir until combined. Remove the pan from the heat. Place the shredded coconut and salt in a food processor and blitz until fine. Add to the pan and stir in. Transfer the mixture to a bowl and place in the fridge for an hour to firm up.

Shape the mixture into walnut-size balls. Place on a baking sheet lined with parchment paper. Freeze for 30 minutes to firm up.

Place the chocolate chips and coconut oil in a pan and melt gently, stirring. Dip each ball into the chocolate with a fork and place back on the tray. Return to the freezer to firm up. Dip the balls in melted chocolate a second time and return to the freezer to set.

The bites will keep in the fridge for 1–2 weeks.

(VE) (GF)

ZUCCHINI AND APPLE CAKE BITES

These delicious green bites are naturally sweetened with apple and have a warming cinnamon flavor reminiscent of zucchini cake. The coconut flour gives a unique texture and helps to bind the mixture.

Place all the ingredients in a food processor and process just until the mixture starts to come together to form a soft dough.

Take walnut-size pieces and roll into balls. Store in the fridge for up to 1 week.

MAKES 14

- ½ cup (60g) grated zucchini
- 2 tbsp applesauce
- ½ apple, grated
- 1 tsp ground cinnamon
- 2 tbsp almond nut butter or other nut butter
- ¼ cup (30g) coconut flour
- ½ cup (50g) rolled oats
- 2 tsp chia seeds
- 1 tsp vanilla extract

PER BITE:

Calories: 46kcal

Fat: 2g
   (0.5g saturated)

Carbohydrates: 4.6g

Sugars: 0.9g

Protein: 1.5g

PECAN PUMPKIN NUGGETS

MAKES 20

- 1 cup (100g) pecans, lightly toasted
- 1 tbsp flaxseed meal
- 1 tbsp ground chia seeds
- ¼ cup (60g) canned pumpkin
- 1 tbsp finely ground xylitol or erythritol
- 1 tbsp yacon syrup, almond milk, or milk
- 1 tbsp lucuma powder (optional)
- 1 tsp maple syrup
- 2 tsp ground cinnamon
- ¼ cup (30g) chocolate chips (vegan if desired)
- Ground cinnamon and xylitol, to coat (optional)

PER BITE:

Calories: 59kcal

Fat: 4.5g
(0.6g saturated)

Carbohydrates: 3g

Sugars: 0.5g

Protein: 1g

The combination of pecans and pumpkin purée with winter spices makes these nuggets perfect fall treats. The yacon syrup gives them a molasses-like taste, but you can omit this and use a dash of milk or almond milk instead to bind.

Place the nuts and seeds in a food processor and process until the nuts are finely ground. Add the remaining ingredients, except the chocolate chips, cinnamon, and xylitol, and process to form a dough.

Add in the chocolate chips and pulse to combine. Take bite-size pieces of the mixture and roll into balls. Dust in cinnamon and xylitol if desired.

Store in the fridge for 1 week.

MAKES 20

½ cup (100g) ready-
to-eat dried figs

1 tbsp vanilla extract

3 tbsp orange juice

Pinch salt

½ cup (50g) rolled
oats

¾ cup (75g) walnuts,
toasted and
chopped

½ cup (60g)
chopped toasted
nuts, to coat

PER BITE:

Calories: 60kcal

Fat: 3.9g
(0.4g saturated)

Carbohydrates: 4.4g

Sugars: 2.8g

Protein: 1.4g

FIG WALNUT BITES

These are similar in taste to fig cookies. As they contain a higher amount of dried fruit than other low-sugar balls in this chapter, they can be used as an energy boost pre- or post-workout.

Place the dried figs with the vanilla, orange juice, and salt in a food processor and blend to form a thick purée. Add the oats and walnuts and process again to form a soft dough. Keep some texture in the mix.

Take bite-size pieces and roll into balls. Roll the balls in the chopped toasted nuts to coat. Store in the fridge for up to 1 week.

CARROT CAKE BITES

MAKES 24

¼ cup (50g) raisins

1 tsp vanilla extract

¼ cup (30g) almond meal or flaxseed meal

1 tbsp xylitol or erythritol

1 cup (60g) unsweetened coconut flakes

1 tbsp coconut oil

½ cup (75g) walnuts

2 tbsp coconut flour

1 tsp ground cinnamon

1 carrot (2½ oz/75g), finely grated

Pinch sea salt

2 tbsp applesauce

PER BITE:

Calories: 66kcal

Fat: 4.8g
(2.1g saturated)

Carbohydrates: 3.6g

Sugars: 2.2g

Protein: 1.2g

Inspired by carrot cake, these delicious little nuggets are creamy and sweet with the addition of applesauce and raisins. Walnuts provide essential omega-3 fats, known to lower inflammation and keep the skin glowing.

Place all the ingredients in a food processor and process to form a dough. Keep some texture in the mixture, so do not overprocess.

Take bite-size pieces of the dough and roll into balls. Store in the fridge for up to 1 week.

For a thoughtful homemade gift, place the bites in a jar, and decorate with a ribbon or handwritten label.

MACA CHOCOLATE TRUFFLE BITES

MAKES 18

½ cup (100ml)
almond milk

½ cup (70g) coconut
oil, softened

5½ oz (150g)
chocolate chips or
grated chocolate
(use sugar-
free, dairy-free
chocolate if you're
vegan)

1 oz (30g) xylitol

1 tbsp maca powder

1 tbsp lucuma
powder

1 tsp vanilla extract

Extra maca or
lucuma powder, to
coat

PER BITE:

Calories: 90kcal

Fat: 6.3g
(4.8g saturated)

Carbohydrates: 7.7g

Sugars: 5.1g

Protein: 0.6g

Give these indulgent treats as a gift instead of a box of chocolates. The bites include maca, a popular superfood that gives you a sustained energy boost through the day. It also supports energy levels and adrenal health. These bites have more sugar than other balls in this chapter, but using xylitol helps to keep the overall sugar content low.

Place the almond milk in a saucepan and bring to a simmer, then turn off the heat. Place all the other ingredients in a blender or food processor. Pour over the hot milk and blend until the mixture becomes a thick, smooth batter. Spoon the mixture into a bowl and chill in the fridge for 1 hour until firm.

Using a spoon, roll the mixture into small truffles. Place the maca or lucuma powder on a plate and roll the truffles in the powder. Place on a plate and keep in the fridge until ready to serve.

These will keep in the fridge for up to 1 week.

PIÑA COLADA ICE-CREAM BITES

MAKES 24

1 cup (250ml) full-fat coconut milk

1½ cups (200g) frozen pineapple pieces

1 tbsp lucuma powder (optional)

1 tsp maca powder (optional)

7 oz (200g) dark chocolate, chopped into small pieces

2 tsp coconut oil

½ cup (50g) dried shredded coconut, to coat

PER BITE:

Calories: 62kcal

Fat: 4g
(2.9g saturated)

Carbohydrates: 5g

Sugars: 1.5g

Protein: 1g

This frozen vegan bite is made with blended coconut cream and pineapple. Maca is known to support our adrenal glands, boosting energy levels and resilience, while lucuma adds natural sweetness and fiber. You could turn these into ice pops by inserting cocktail sticks into the center of each one before freezing.

Line a shallow baking pan or plastic container with parchment paper.

Place the coconut milk, frozen pineapple, and powders, if using, in a blender or food processor and blend to a thick soft cream. Pour into the container and place in the freezer for 1 hour until firm but not too hard.

Melt the chocolate in a pan with the coconut oil. Place the shredded coconut on a plate.

Remove the mixture from the freezer and slice into small squares. Dip these into the chocolate, coating all sides. Coat the squares with the coconut, then place back on the parchment paper. Store in the freezer for up to 3 months. Best eaten frozen.

(VE) (GF)

GINGERBREAD NUGGETS

A perfect treat for the fall months, these lightly spiced nuggets are naturally rich in protein thanks to the garbanzo beans – this may sound like an odd addition, but it creates a lovely creamy texture.

Place all the ingredients in a food processor and blend to form a chunky paste, but keep a little texture in the mixture.

Take spoonfuls of the mixture and shape into little balls. Roll in the cinnamon and stevia to coat.

Place in the fridge for 30 minutes to firm before eating. Store in the fridge for up to 1 week.

MAKES 24

14 oz (400g) can garbanzos, drained
¼ cup (30g) flaxseed meal
1 tsp granulated stevia or xylitol
½ cup (60g) pecans
2 tbsp almond nut butter or other nut butter
1 tsp vanilla extract
½ tsp ground ginger
¼ cup (40g) stem ginger
1 tsp ground cinnamon
Granulated stevia mixed with 1 tsp ground cinnamon, to coat

PER BITE:
Calories: 53kcal
**Fat: 3.3g
(0.3g saturated)**
Carbohydrates: 3.5g
Sugars: 1.3g
Protein: 1.6g

MOCHA BREAKFAST OATMEAL BITES

These coffee-flavored bites are a great grab-and-go breakfast option. Naturally sweetened with banana, they are also packed with fiber to help stabilize blood sugar levels.

Place the oats, flaxseed, coffee, and cacao powder in a food processor and briefly process to combine. Add the remaining ingredients and process until the mixture comes together to form a soft dough. Try not to overprocess so you keep some texture.

Take small walnut-size pieces of the dough and roll into balls. Dust in a little ground coffee mixed with cacao powder if desired.

Refrigerate the bites until ready to serve. They will keep for at least 1 week in the fridge.

MAKES 18

½ cup (50g) rolled oats

¼ cup (30g) flaxseed meal or chia seeds

2 tsp ground coffee (instant or fresh)

¼ cup (30g) raw cacao powder

1 tbsp vanilla extract

¼ cup (75g) tahini

½ large banana

Pinch sea salt

Ground coffee mixed with cacao powder, to coat (optional)

PER BITE:

Calories: 58kcal

Fat: 3.5g
    (0.5g saturated)

Carbohydrates: 3.9g

Sugars: 0.6g

Protein: 1.9g

WHITE CHOCOLATE BERRY TRUFFLES

MAKES 14

¾ cup (125g) white chocolate chips

1 tbsp unsalted butter, softened

1 tbsp coconut cream or heavy cream

1 tbsp xylitol (optional)

Few drops berry fruit flavoring extract

¼ cup (40g) fresh pitted cherries or other fresh berries

½ cup (60g) almond meal or protein powder (vanilla or berry flavor)

Berry powder or crushed freeze-dried berries, for rolling (optional)

Best eaten semi-frozen, you can use any fresh berries in the recipe. Fruit flavoring extracts are now widely available and really help to intensify the berry flavor. Do not use frozen berries as they are too wet. If you'd like to reduce the sugar content further, use a low-sugar white chocolate.

Place the chocolate, butter, coconut cream, and xylitol, if using, in a pan, and gently melt, stirring continuously. Transfer to a blender or food processor, add the rest of the ingredients, and process until smooth and creamy.

Chill the mixture for 3–4 hours or freeze for 1 hour to harden.

Take spoonfuls of the mixture and roll into balls. Dust in a little berry powder or freeze-dried berries, if desired, to serve. Store in the fridge for 1–2 weeks or freeze for up to 3 months.

PER BITE:

Calories: 97kcal

Fat: 8g
  (3.7g saturated)

Carbohydrates: 4.8g

Sugars: 2.7g

Protein: 1.2g

KEY LIME PIE BITES

MAKES 18

- 1 oz (30g) xylitol or ½ oz (15g) granulated stevia
- ¾ cup (125g) macadamia nuts
- ½ cup (35g) dried shredded coconut
- 2 tsp wheatgrass powder or supergreens powder
- Zest and juice of 1 lime
- Pinch sea salt
- 1 tsp coconut oil, softened
- Powdered xylitol mixed with a little lime zest, to coat

PER BITE:
Calories: 73kcal
Fat: 6.6g
  (1.8g saturated)
Carbohydrates: 2.1g
Sugars: 0.4g
Protein: 0.9g

Lime and coconut is a delicious combination. The sharpness of the lime is a wonderful contrast to the creamy texture of these little bites. Macadamia nuts are packed with anti-inflammatory fats and rich in B vitamins, manganese, and magnesium, which are all important for energy production.

Place the xylitol in a food processor and blend until really fine. Add the nuts and coconut and continue to process until fine.

Add the green powder, lime zest and juice, and sea salt and process until the mixture forms a soft dough. Add the coconut oil to help the mixture come together.

Scoop out bite-size pieces and roll into balls. Roll in the powdered xylitol mixed with lime zest.

Store the balls in the fridge until ready to serve, or keep them in the freezer for up to 3 months.

PEANUT CRISPIES

These are similar to the traditional children's favorite, chocolate crispies, but much better for you. Yacon syrup is a healthier sweetener with a lower glycemic index and high content of the dietary fiber inulin, making it ideal for supporting digestive health. If you can't get hold of it, use rice malt syrup instead. Any nut butter can be used instead of peanut butter.

Gently heat the coconut oil, yacon syrup, and peanut butter in a saucepan and stir until melted. Turn off the heat. Add the cacao powder, coconut, and puffed rice and stir well to coat.

Scoop out spoonfuls of the mixture, shape into small balls using two teaspoons, and place into mini paper cases. Refrigerate for 1 hour until set. These will keep in the fridge for 1–2 weeks.

MAKES 24

¼ cup (60g) coconut oil

¼ cup (50g) yacon syrup or rice malt syrup

¼ cup (60g) peanut butter or other nut butter

¼ cup (30g) raw cacao powder

½ cup (40g) dried shredded coconut

2 cups (30g) puffed rice cereal

PER BITE:

Calories: 64kcal

Fat: 5g
  (3.4g saturated)

Carbohydrates: 2.9g

Sugars: 0.7g

Protein: 1.2g

PISTACHIO CRANBERRY BITES

MAKES 36

1 cup (125g) shelled
pistachio nuts

1 tbsp ground chia
seeds

1 oz (30g) xylitol or
erythritol

½ cup (60g)
almonds

½ cup (100g)
almond nut butter
or other nut butter

1 tbsp vanilla extract

½ cup (60g) dried
cranberries

PER BITE:

Calories: 58kcal

Fat: 4.4g
(0.6g saturated)

Carbohydrates: 2.2g

Sugars: 1.5g

Protein: 2g

These delicious nutty bites are rich in protein and healthy fats. Use any nut butter you like but try to choose one without additives and sweeteners. Pistachios are a great source of monounsaturated heart-healthy fats, vitamin E, and carotenes, helping to contribute to glowing skin.

Place the pistachios, chia seeds, xylitol, and almonds in a food processor and process until fine. Add the nut butter, vanilla, and half the cranberries and continue to process until the mixture comes together. Add the remaining cranberries and pulse to break up.

Take pieces of the dough and roll into little balls. Store them in the fridge until ready to serve. The bites will keep for 1–2 weeks.

BLACKCURRANT BLISS BITES

MAKES 14

½ cup (60g) walnuts

½ cup (60g) pecans

¼ cup (30g) raw
cacao powder

1 tbsp freeze-dried
blackcurrant
powder or other
berry powder

Pinch sea salt

1 tbsp blueberry
or cherry juice
concentrate

¼ cup (50g) Greek
yogurt

Crushed nuts, to coat
(optional)

PER BITE:

Calories: 80kcal

Fat: 6.6g
(0.9g saturated)

Carbohydrates: 2.8g

Sugars: 1.1g

Protein: 1.8g

Blackcurrants are a seasonal fruit, but you can find freeze-dried blackcurrant powder (and other berry powders) any time of year – a great way to add flavor, antioxidants, and vitamin C. These bites are sweetened with a little blueberry or cherry concentrate – if unavailable, you could use applesauce. The walnuts add plant-based omega-3 fats along with protein and give these balls a rich taste when combined with the raw cacao powder.

Place the walnuts, pecans, and cacao powder in a food processor and combine until the nuts are finely ground. Add the blackcurrant powder and sea salt, then pour in the juice and yogurt and process to combine.

Take teaspoons of the mixture and roll into small balls. Roll in crushed nuts if desired. Store in the fridge for up to 1 week.

ABOUT THE AUTHORS

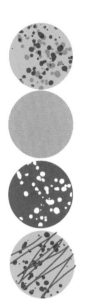

Christine Bailey is a qualified nutritionist, chef, presenter, and the author of over 13 recipe and health books. She makes regular appearances in the media, including BBC's *The Truth About Sugar*, BBC's *The Truth About Stress,* and Sky News. For more information, see christinebailey.co.uk.

Heather Thomas is a food writer and editor, and the author of several best-selling health and cooking books, including *The Avocado Cookbook* and *The Greek Vegetarian Cookbook*. She has worked with many top chefs and women's health organizations, and has contributed to health and food magazines in the UK and the United States.

Thunder Bay Press
An imprint of Printers Row Publishing Group
9717 Pacific Heights Blvd, San Diego, CA 92121
www.thunderbaybooks.com • mail@thunderbaybooks.com

Printers Row Publishing Group is a division of Readerlink Distribution Services, LLC.
Thunder Bay Press is a registered trademark of Readerlink Distribution Services, LLC.

Correspondence regarding the content of this book should be sent to Thunder Bay Press, Editorial Department, at the above address. Author or rights inquiries should be addressed to Elwin Street Productions at the below address.

Thunder Bay Press
Publisher: Peter Norton • Associate Publisher: Ana Parker
Editor: Dan Mansfield
Acquisitions Editor: Kathryn Chipinka Dalby

Conceived and produced by
Elwin Street Productions
10 Elwin Street
London E2 7BU
United Kingdom

Illustrations by Moira Clinch
Photographs by Uyen Luu: 4, 34, 57, 67, 109, 115, 117, 123, 127, 129, 135, 139, 141, 143
All other photographs are from Shutterstock

Library of Congress Control Number: 2021946066

ISBN: 978-1-64517-947-4

Printed in the United Arab Emirates

25 24 23 22 21 1 2 3 4 5